Health and safety in care homes

HSE Books

© Crown copyright 2014

First published 2001

Second edition 2014

ISBN 978 0 7176 6368 2

You may reuse this information (not including logos) free of charge in any format or medium, under the terms of the Open Government Licence. To view the licence visit www.nationalarchives.gov.uk/doc/open-government-licence, write to the Information Policy Team, The National Archives, Kew, London TW9 4DU, or email psi@nationalarchives.gsi.gov.uk.

Some images and illustrations may not be owned by the Crown so cannot be reproduced without permission of the copyright owner. Enquiries should be sent to copyright@hse.gsi.gov.uk.

This guidance is issued by the Health and Safety Executive. Following the guidance is not compulsory, unless specifically stated, and you are free to take other action. But if you do follow the guidance you will normally be doing enough to comply with the law. Health and safety inspectors seek to secure compliance with the law and may refer to this guidance.

Health and Safety Executive

Contents

Introduction 1

The regulation of health and safety in care homes   1

Chapter 1   Managing health and safety   3

Key legislation   3
What you need to do   3
   Plan: Say what you want to happen   4
   Do: Make sure systems are in place to provide the tools and equipment to do the job safely   4
   Check: Make sure work is being done safely   6
   Act: Learn from problems and successes, and make improvements   6
   Other considerations   6
Key points to consider   7

Chapter 2   Reporting of incidents   9

Key legislation   9
What needs to be reported to the RIDDOR enforcing authority, and by when?   9
Who should report and how?   10
Should records be kept, and can they be shared with staff?   10
Key points to consider   11

Chapter 3   Moving and handling   12

Key legislation   12
What you need to do   12
   Moving and handling arrangements   12
   Moving and handling equipment   14
   Training   16
Key points to consider   16

Chapter 4   Equipment safety   17

Key legislation   17
Role of the Medicines and Healthcare products Regulatory Agency   17
What you need to do   17
   Provision and Use of Work Equipment Regulations 1998 (PUWER)   17
   Lifting Operations and Lifting Equipment Regulations 1998 (LOLER)   17
   Electrical safety   19
Key points to consider   20

Chapter 5   Safe use of bed rails   22

Key legislation   22
What you need to do   22
   Ensuring the correct use of bed rails   22
   Entrapment underneath the rail   23
   Entrapment between the end of the rail and the headboard or footboard   24
   Entrapment between the bed rail and the side of the mattress   25
   Risk of falls when using bed rails   26
Key points to consider   26

Chapter 6 Slips, trips and falls on the level 27

Key legislation 27
What you need to do 27
   Controlling the risk 27
     Environmental factors 28
     Organisational factors 28
Key points to consider 28

Chapter 7 Falls from height 30

Key legislation 30
What you need to do 30
   Controlling the risks to residents 30
   Controlling the risks to employees 31
Key points to consider 32

Chapter 8 Hazardous substances, infections and diseases 34

Key legislation 34
What you need to do 34
   Specific hazardous substances, infections and diseases 35
   Infection prevention and control 36
   Medicines and drugs 37
Key points to consider 38

Chapter 9 Legionella 40

Key legislation 40
What you need to do 40
   Management of legionella (example checklist) 41
Key points to consider 42

Chapter 10 Hot water and surfaces 44

Key legislation 44
What you need to do 44
  Hot water 45
  Hot surfaces 45
Key points to consider 45

Chapter 11 Work-related violence and aggression 47

Key legislation 47
What you need to do 47
  The general risks 48
  The risks from individuals 48
  Information and training 49
Helping staff after an incident 49
Key points to consider 50

Chapter 12 Work-related stress 51

Key legislation 51
What you need to do 51
  Examples of how you might tackle stress at work 52
Key points to consider 53

Chapter 13 General work environment 54

Key legislation 54
What you need to do 54
   Asbestos 54
   Radon 55
   Gas safety 55
   Fire safety 56
   Contractors 56
   Outside areas and vehicle movements 57
   Doors and gates 57
   Ventilation and heating 58
   Display screen equipment (DSE) 58
Key points to consider 59

Chapter 14 General welfare 60

Key legislation 60
What you need to do 60
   Staff welfare facilities 60
   Smoking 61
   Working time 61
   New and expectant mothers 62
   First aid 63
Key points to consider 64

Appendix 1 Legal framework 65

The Health and Safety at Work etc Act 1974 (HSWA) 65

Further information 66

Introduction

Care homes differ from other workplaces because they are not only places of work but are also homes for their residents. It is therefore important that they are pleasant places where the freedom and dignity of residents is respected, and where everyone's health and safety is sensibly and effectively managed.

They are owned and managed by a wide range of organisations, including local authorities, the NHS, and those from the private and voluntary sectors. This guidance is aimed at owners, providers and managers. It will also help safety representatives carry out their roles and responsibilities and may be of interest to employees.

It describes the main health and safety risks found in care homes, and what should be done to protect both workers and those receiving care. Each chapter can be read in isolation, and has a 'Find out more' section, providing details of further information from the Health and Safety Executive (HSE) or other organisations.

At the end of each chapter there is a short list of key questions. This is not an exhaustive list, but is intended to help prompt your thinking about whether you are complying with the law and what more you might need to do.

For ease of reading, the term 'resident' is used throughout to refer to users of a service in a care home (eg patients, older people, and people with learning disabilities or mental health problems).

The regulation of health and safety in care homes

This guidance has been revised during a period of change. At the time of publication (June 2014), HSE and local authorities investigate serious worker and resident incidents. Under the Enforcing Authority Regulations, HSE regulates homes with nursing and local authority owned or run care homes. Other homes are regulated by local authorities.

It is anticipated, however, that the Care Quality Commission (CQC) in England will soon become the lead investigator of incidents where residents have been harmed because of unsafe or poor quality care. The roles of other regulators are also being reviewed.

Appropriate standards will remain the same, irrespective of which regulator investigates and enforces following cases of unsafe care. So this publication concentrates on providing practical guidance and does not provide extensive legal referencing, apart from short 'Key legislation' sections in each chapter.

However, Appendix 1 provides a brief summary of duties under the Health and Safety at Work etc Act 1974 (the HSWA), including those on directors and senior managers. The general requirements of section 3 of the HSWA apply to all sections of the guidance that deal with resident or public safety. There is also a brief summary of duties under the Working Time Regulations in Chapter 14.

Other changes in regulation across Great Britain are also being considered and future editions will reflect these changes.

This edition does not cover the following issues:

- standards relating to quality of care. These are regulated by the CQC (in England), the Care Inspectorate (in Scotland) and the Care and Social Services Inspectorate Wales;
- the conduct and performance of registered health and social care professionals. These are regulated by various professional councils;
- safeguarding arrangements to protect vulnerable people from abuse or neglect. Local authorities take the lead role for safeguarding.

Chapter 1 Managing health and safety

1.1 Social care is about people – a large, diverse workforce looking after a predominantly vulnerable population. Employees have the right to work in a healthy and safe workplace, while residents should receive care that is safe, and takes their needs, freedoms and dignity into account.

1.2 Managing these different needs will sometimes present unique and complex situations which can, when not effectively managed, result in serious harm to employees or residents. You need to be aware of the different risks and control them effectively.

Key legislation

- Health and Safety at Work etc Act 1974
- Management of Health and Safety at Work Regulations 1999

What you need to do

1.3 Good management of health and safety does not happen on its own. You will already have management processes to deal with payroll, personnel and finances. Managing for health and safety is no different and should be an integral part of the everyday running of your care home, and of the behaviours and attitudes displayed by all.

1.4 The core elements that are required to help you manage for health and safety are:

- good leadership and management;
- a trained and skilled (competent) workforce;
- an environment where people are consulted and feel involved.

1.5 To help you determine if you are doing enough to manage health and safety, consider the following questions:

- How does the home demonstrate its commitment to health and safety?
- Are your arrangements to control the real risks people are facing working?
- How well do you know what is happening in the home – are there effective checks in place?
- Have you learned from situations where things have gone wrong?
- Is health and safety an integral part of your day-to-day process for running your care home?

1.6 Managing for health and safety requires a sustained and systematic approach. While this may not always require a formal health and safety management system, your approach is likely to follow the steps Plan, Do, Check and Act:

- **Plan:** say what needs to happen and say how you will achieve it.
- **Do:** profile the risks you identify, organise your activities to deliver your plan, decide on the preventive measures, and ensure there are systems and equipment in place to do the job safely.

- **Check:** monitor the work to see if it's being done safely and investigate the causes of accidents, incidents or near misses.
- **Act:** review your performance and take action on lessons learned, including from audit and inspection reports.

Plan: Say what you want to happen

Write a health and safety policy
1.7 Set out your arrangements for managing health and safety in the home to let staff and others know your commitment. Your health and safety policy does not need to be long or complicated, but it should clearly say who does what, when and how.

Decide who will help you with you duties
1.8 To help you meet your health and safety duties, you can appoint someone who is competent. A competent person is not someone who simply has the competence to carry out a particular task safely. In general terms, the definition of a competent person is someone who has the necessary skills, experience and knowledge to manage health and safety.

1.9 To help you manage the health risks to employees, using an occupational health service can help you identify risks, advise on suitable precautions and control measures, and provide services such as:

- health surveillance programmes;
- feedback and advice to employers following employee health assessments, eg pre-employment, following sickness absence, or rehabilitation and return to work;
- clinical services such as immunisations;
- employee information and training in the health aspects of their work.

Consult with your employees
1.10 You must consult your employees, in good time, on health and safety issues. This is a two-way process, as it allows staff to raise concerns and influence decisions on health and safety management. Issues you should consult employees on include:

- risks arising from their work;
- proposals to manage and/or control these risks;
- the best ways of providing information and training.

1.11 If you recognise a trade union, consultation will be through appointed health and safety representatives. In non-unionised workplaces, you can consult either directly or through other elected representatives or a combination of the two.

Do: Make sure systems are in place to provide the tools and equipment to do the job safely

Control the risks
1.12 Assess the risks and decide whether you are doing enough to prevent harm to people. Decide what the priorities are and identify the biggest risks. The typical hazards found in a social care setting are all covered in this publication.

1.13 Risk assessment is not about creating huge amounts of paperwork, it's about:

- identifying the significant hazards;
- deciding who might be harmed and how;

- evaluating the risks and deciding on precautions;
- recording your significant findings;
- reviewing assessments and updating as necessary.

1.14 You may need to consider different elements of risk, including:

- the common risks to everyone on the premises, eg risks from legionella, asbestos, electrical equipment, challenging behaviour and moving vehicles;
- common risks to residents, eg risks from falls from height or scalding, and general precautions capable of preventing harm to the most vulnerable;
- risks to workers arising from the tasks they undertake, eg moving and handling residents, responding to challenging behaviour, using hazardous substances, maintenance activities etc;
- risks to particular staff, eg expectant mothers, young employees, or those with pre-existing injuries which may impact on work;
- risks to particular residents, eg the risk of them falling out of bed or needing help with bathing or to move around safely.

1.15 Individual risk assessments may be integrated into 'care assessments' or 'support plans' that may be required by other regulators. The important point is to ensure that you have considered the individual's needs and how these can be delivered safely.

Making sensible risk assessment decisions
1.16 When considering the care needs of an individual, everyday activities are often identified that will benefit their lives, but also put them at some level of risk. This requires a balanced decision to be made between the needs, freedom and dignity of the individual and their safety – with the aim of enabling residents to live fulfilled lives safely, rather than providing reasons for restricting them.

1.17 A person-centred approach, working with the resident, family and professionals involved, may help achieve the outcomes that matter to the resident. Discussing capacity will help the resident think through the possible consequences, positive or negative, of any action or inaction. This enables everyone involved to explore the issues, make informed choices and accept responsibilities. Arrangements can then be provided which go as far as possible towards meeting the individual's aspirations, while recognising their limitations and managing any risks to themselves and others.

1.18 Key points to consider when balancing risk include:

- concentrating on real risks that could actually cause harm;
- close liaison with the resident, carer and family/representative when carrying out risk assessments, which is essential to achieve outcomes that matter to them;
- how the risks flowing from a resident's choice can best be reduced, so far as reasonably practicable, by putting sensible controls in place, eg when organising group activities, thinking how the most vulnerable can be protected without unnecessarily restricting the freedoms of the most capable.

Provide information and training
1.19 Provide clear instructions, information and adequate training for your employees. Everyone who works for you needs to know how to work safely and without risks to health. Pay particular attention to:

- the induction and training of new employees (permanent and temporary), young workers, and nightshift employees;

- those given specific responsibilities under your health and safety arrangements;
- the need to review training, if tasks/equipment change or staff are changing jobs or taking on extra responsibilities.

Check: Make sure the work is being done safely

1.20 Check that you are controlling the risks in your organisation. This is a vital, sometimes overlooked step. It will give you the confidence that you are doing enough to keep on top of health and safety, and may show you how you could do things better in the future.

1.21 Check that staff are following arrangements you have set up, as well as investigating and analysing incidents. The 'Key points to consider' at the end of each chapter may provide the basis of a monitoring system to help you meet your needs.

Act: Learn from problems and successes, and make improvements

1.22 Revisit your plans to confirm whether your health and safety arrangements are still appropriate and are achieving what you wanted them to achieve. This should enable you to see:

- what has changed;
- what you can stop doing;
- any new things you need to start doing.

Other considerations

Employment status
1.23 If you use temporary (agency) workers, it is important to be clear about their employment status, as employers have particular health and safety duties to their employees. Although the employment business may be their legal employer, you will also have responsibilities for them while they are on your premises.

1.24 In practice, employment businesses should ensure that health and safety responsibilities are clearly assigned and based on the particular facts of the employment relationship. Where different organisations share responsibility for managing staff, the temporary worker's employer is responsible for ensuring adequate arrangements are in place for health and safety.

Migrant workers
1.25 If you employ migrant workers in your care home, you will need to consider:

- language, communication and cultural differences;
- basic competencies, such as literacy and numeracy;
- general health, and relevant work experience;
- whether vocational qualifications are compatible with those in Great Britain;
- the possible effects of the attitudes and assumptions of workers new to work in Great Britain, or of British workers or residents towards them.

1.26 As well as the duty to ensure that risks to migrant workers are being managed, care homes must also take steps to ensure that the safety of residents is protected, for example by ensuring:

- competence in new and unfamiliar equipment and procedures;
- that work instructions and different clinical practices are understood;
- that there is effective communication, both between employees and between employees and residents.

Young or vulnerable workers

1.27 If you employ young people under 18, you should take account of:

- inexperience, lack of awareness of risks and immaturity of young people;
- the workplace and equipment;
- the nature and degree of exposure to harm;
- organisation of processes and activities;
- the level of training they have received;
- risks from specified processes and chemical, physical or biological agents (see www.hse.gov.uk/youngpeople/law).

Key points to consider

Plan

- Have you thought about what you want to achieve, how to do this and who will be responsible for what?
- Does everyone understand their roles and responsibilities towards health and safety?
- Do you have access to competent advice?
- Do you understand the risks in your workplace?

Do

- Have you assessed the risks?
- Have you put suitable control measures in place?
- Are there arrangements for consulting with employees and their representatives?
- Are staff suitably trained?

Check

- Are you checking how well risks are being controlled in practice?
- Do you monitor health and safety performance, actively (eg spot checks) and reactively (eg accident and near-miss investigations)?

Act

- Have you reviewed your health and safety performance?
- Have you taken action on lessons learned from incidents, inspections and other monitoring?
- Have you revisited your policies and plan to see if they need updating?

Find out more

Health and safety made simple: The basics for your business Leaflet INDG449 HSE Books www.hse.gov.uk/pubns/indg449.htm
Microsite: www.hse.gov.uk/simple-health-safety

The health and safety toolbox: How to control risks at work HSG268 HSE Books ISBN 978 0 7176 6587 7 www.hse.gov.uk/pubns/books/hsg268.htm
Microsite: www.hse.gov.uk/toolbox

Managing for health and safety HSG65 (Third edition) HSE Books 2013 ISBN 978 0 7176 6456 6 www.hse.gov.uk/pubns/books/hsg65.htm

HSE's 'Managing for health and safety' website: www.hse.gov.uk/managing

HSE's risk management site: www.hse.gov.uk/risk

HSE advice on migrant workers: www.hse.gov.uk/migrantworkers

Advice on young people at work: www.hse.gov.uk/youngpeople

Chapter 2 Reporting of incidents

2.1 Incidents and near misses at work can provide an indication of how well health and safety is being managed, and recording such incidents allows others to learn from them. Certain incidents are required by law to be reported to the appropriate enforcing authority.

Key legislation

- Reporting of Injuries, Diseases and Dangerous Occurrences Regulations 2013 (RIDDOR)

2.2 There are a number of reporting requirements administered by other regulators in social care, eg notification requirements under the Care Quality Commission (Registration) Regulations 2009. These requirements are separate to and distinct from the legal duty to report incidents under RIDDOR.

What needs to be reported to the RIDDOR enforcing authority, and by when?

2.3 The following are reportable, if they arise 'out of or in connection with work':

- The death of any person, whether or not they are at work, must be reported **without delay**, using the quickest means. A report must be received within ten days of the accident.
- Accidents which result in an employee or a self-employed person suffering a specified injury (as defined by RIDDOR) must be reported **without delay**, using the quickest means. A report must have been received within ten days of the accident.
- Accidents which result in an employee or a self-employed person being absent from work or unable to do their normal duties for more than seven days must be reported **within fifteen days** of the incident.
- Accidents which result in a person not at work (eg a patient, resident or visitor) suffering an injury and being taken to a hospital for treatment must be reported **without delay**, using the quickest means. A report must have been received within ten days of the accident. If an accident happens at a hospital, and the person receives a specified injury, it is the hospital's duty to report it.
- An employee or self-employed person must report diagnoses of certain occupational diseases, where these are likely to have been caused or made worse by their work.
- Specified dangerous occurrences (as defined by RIDDOR), which may not result in a reportable injury but have the potential to do significant harm, must be reported without delay using the quickest possible means. A report must have been received **within ten days** of the incident.

2.4 You can find more detail on specified injuries, occupational diseases, dangerous occurrences and examples of what should be reported under RIDDOR in HSE's information sheet *Reporting injuries, diseases and dangerous occurrences in health and social care: Guidance for employers* (HSIS1) – see 'Find out more' on page 11.

Who should report and how?

2.5 The duty to notify and report rests with the 'responsible person'. This may be the employer of an injured person, a self-employed person or someone in control of premises where work is carried out. See Table 1 for more information.

Table 1 The responsible person for reporting incidents

Reportable incident	Injured person	Responsible person
Death, specified injury, over-seven-day injury or case of disease	An employee at work	That person's employer
Death, specified injury or over-seven-day injury	A self-employed person at work in premises under the control of someone else	The person in control of the premises
Specified injury, over-seven-day injury or case of disease	A self-employed person at work in premises under their control	The self-employed person or someone acting on their behalf
Death or injury requiring removal to hospital for treatment (or major injury occurring at a hospital)	A person not at work (but affected by the work of someone else), eg patient, volunteer or visitor	The person in control of the premises or in domestic premises the employer in control of the work activity
Dangerous occurrence		The person in control of the premises where (or in connection with the work at which) the dangerous occurrence happened

2.6 Death, specified injury and over-seven-day injuries to agency staff and contractors working indirectly for you are reportable by their employers.

2.7 All incidents can be reported online (www.hse.gov.uk/riddor) but a telephone service remains for reporting **fatal and specified injuries only**. Call the Incident Contact Centre on 0845 300 9923 (opening hours Monday to Friday 8.30 am to 5 pm).

Should records be kept, and can they be shared with staff?

2.8 You must keep a record of any reportable injury, disease or dangerous occurrence for three years. This must include:

- the date and method of reporting;
- the date, time and place of the event;
- personal details of those involved;
- a brief description of the nature of the event or disease.

2.9 You must also keep records of over-three-day injuries to your employees, although these are not reportable until the employee is off work for more than seven days.

2.10 You must make relevant health and safety documents available to safety representatives. This includes records kept under RIDDOR, except where they reveal personal health information about individuals.

Key points to consider

- Do your staff report incidents, including near misses?
- Are all reportable incidents being reported through RIDDOR?
- Do you have an accident book and do you keep a record of any reportable injury, disease or dangerous occurrence for three years?
- Do you investigate incidents to learn lessons and take action, eg by reviewing risk assessments and safe working procedures?

Find out more

HSE's health and social care RIDDOR webpage:
www.hse.gov.uk/healthservices/riddor.htm

HSE's RIDDOR site: www.hse.gov.uk/riddor

Reporting injuries, diseases and dangerous occurrences in health and social care: Guidance for employers HSIS1(rev1) HSE 2013 www.hse.gov.uk/pubns/hsis1.htm

Chapter 3 Moving and handling

3.1 Helping residents is a key part of the working day for most care home employees. A significant number of injuries to staff are caused by moving and handling people. Some residents may need assistance to move around safely and to participate in activities, others may be dependent on staff for bathing, dressing and other tasks which involve moving and handling.

3.2 Poor moving and handling practices can lead to:

- back pain and musculoskeletal disorders, which can result in disability and people being unable to work;
- accidents, which can injure both the employee and the resident being moved;
- discomfort and a lack of dignity for the resident.

3.3 Work in care homes can also involve many other handling tasks, such as lifting, moving, putting down, pushing, pulling and carrying loads and equipment in laundry, kitchen, stores cleaning and maintenance activities. These also need to be managed to reduce the risk of injury and musculoskeletal disorders.

Key legislation

- Manual Handling Operations Regulations 1992
- Provision and Use of Work Equipment Regulations 1998 (PUWER)

What you need to do

3.4 Assessing moving and handling risks can usually be done in-house, as long as people are competent to identify and address the risks. You may need to seek specialist advice on how to assist some residents with specific moving and handling needs. Sources of advice include:

- occupational therapists and physiotherapists;
- manual handling advisers and ergonomists with experience in health and social care;
- professional bodies and organisations, such as the National Back Exchange or Chartered Society for Physiotherapists (see 'Find out more' at the end of the chapter).

Moving and handling arrangements

3.5 Things you will need to consider when looking at your overall moving and handling requirements within the care home include:

- the type and frequency of moving and handling tasks;
- the range and amount of equipment needed, equipment storage and maintenance;
- staff required for moving and handling, and their competence and training;
- the environment, eg flooring, ramps, lighting, space restrictions etc;
- moving and handling in the event of emergencies, such as fire evacuations, residents' falls etc.

Person-centred assessments

3.6 You should consider the needs of specific residents as part of the care planning process. Take a balanced approach to managing the safety of employees alongside residents' reasonable expectations of autonomy, privacy and dignity. Where possible, you should have input from the resident and/or their family so they are involved in choices over how their needs are met, are reassured about the safety and comfort of the equipment, and understand how it will help prevent injury to themselves and those caring for them. This information should be communicated to staff and kept accessible for easy reference.

3.7 The risk assessment and care plan for an individual resident should adequately cover their moving and handling needs, both day and night, including:

- what the resident is able/unable to do independently;
- the extent of the resident's ability to support their own weight and any other relevant factors, eg pain, disability, spasm, fatigue, tissue viability or tendency to fall;
- the extent to which the resident can participate in/cooperate with transfers;
- whether the resident needs assistance to reposition themselves/sit up when in their bed/chair and how this will be achieved, eg provision of an electric profiling bed;
- the specific equipment to be used, including (if applicable) type of bed, bath and chair as well as specific handling equipment, ie type of hoist and sling, sling size and which attachments are to be used;
- the assistance required for different types of transfer, including the number of staff needed. Hoisting tasks may require more than one worker to assist in safe transfer;
- moving and handling in the event of emergencies, such as fire evacuations, residents' falls etc.

3.8 Residents' needs and abilities can change over the course of a day. Some residents may become upset or agitated when being moved, and others although willing to assist at the start of a manoeuvre may suddenly find themselves unable to continue. Injuries have occurred to both staff and residents in such circumstances. Staff should be aware of these factors and the impact they may have on moving and handling practices, and be trained in how to deal with them.

Load handling assessments

3.9 It is important not to forget that there can be significant 'non-people' handling risks in a care home. Common areas where manual handling occurs include the laundry, kitchen, stores, cleaning and maintenance. You will need to consider:

- the type and frequency of moving and handling tasks;
- the range of equipment needed;
- the environment, eg flooring, ramps, lighting, space restrictions etc;
- staff required for moving and handling tasks.

3.10 You should identify how to reduce the risk of injury to the lowest level reasonably practicable. This is often through simple and inexpensive means, such as changing the layout of a store or laundry room, or using suitable height trolleys.

3.11 Give particular consideration to employees who are pregnant (or have been recently), and those who are known to have injuries or ill health. You may need to reassess the task, equipment provided or organisation of the work, or consider redeployment to other tasks. Where needed, seek advice from an occupational health specialist.

Moving and handling equipment

3.12 This section should be read in conjunction with Chapter 4 'Equipment safety'.

3.13 The types and amount of equipment needed will vary according to the dependency and specific needs of residents. Equipment typically can include:

- a selection of hoists, eg bariatric hoists, hoists to raise fallen residents from the floor, standing aids, mobile hoists, bath hoists or lifts, adjustable height baths etc;
- slings of different types and sizes to meet residents' needs;
- slide sheets and transfer boards;
- turntables;
- electric profiling beds – for dependent/immobile residents;
- wheelchairs;
- handling belts to assist weight-bearing residents (not for lifting);
- lifting cushions;
- support rails/poles;
- emergency evacuation equipment;
- suitable walking aids, hand rails etc for mobile residents needing minor assistance.

3.14 Equipment should only be introduced following an assessment, and should be used in conjunction with the care plan and the manufacturer's instructions.

Use of hoists and slings

3.15 The number of staff required for hoisting can vary, depending on the needs of the individual resident and the specific hoisting transfers required. Some can safely use a hoist without assistance, others may need assistance from a number of staff. You should ensure your assessment considers:

- the resident being assisted, and their needs;
- the environment;
- specific hoisting transfers;
- equipment provided;
- how the sling is to be applied;
- the individuals who are carrying out the moving and handling tasks.

3.16 In some cases, assessment will show that at least two carers are needed – one to operate the hoist, and the other to help keep the individual in a safe position while moving, to maintain cooperation and provide direct reassurance.

3.17 Safe working procedures must be followed during hoisting. Failure to do so can result in serious or fatal accidents. Problems may include:

- selecting the wrong type of hoist or sling. This can result in inadequate support and the risk of falling from the sling. For example, toileting slings give good access, but little support, so their use should be restricted to toileting only;
- selecting the wrong-size sling, resulting in discomfort if the sling is too small, or the risk of a person slipping through the sling if it is too large. Staff should be aware that sling sizes and coding vary between manufacturers;
- selecting the wrong loops. Slings may come with a range of different length loops for attaching to the hoist. The length of attachment determines how reclined or upright a resident is during the lift. Incorrect selection of loops for an individual may mean they are at risk of slipping out of the sling;

- incompatibility of the hoist and sling, resulting in insecure attachment between the two. Always follow the manufacturer's advice. Concerns about sling/hoist design, supply, instructions or compatibility should be referred to the Medicines and Healthcare products Regulatory Agency (MHRA) at www.mhra.gov.uk;
- failure to use a safety harness, belt or attachment where the sling has one;
- failure due to lack of maintenance/inspection. See Chapter 4 'Equipment safety';
- hoist overturn due to manoeuvring over difficult ground, or not following manufacturer's instructions for use;
- leaving a vulnerable person unattended in a hoist, or just prior to hoisting, in a position where they are likely to fall.

Use of electric profiling beds (EPBs)

3.18 Using EPBs can greatly reduce the risk of musculoskeletal disorders and back pain in employees who assist residents to move in bed. They can also enhance comfort and independence for those who use them, and reduce the risk of pressure damage.

3.19 Where there is a significant risk of injury, because a resident requires regular moving and handling in bed, providing an EPB will be a reasonably practicable control measure. Examples of moving and handling tasks where the risk of injury is significantly reduced by using EPBs include:

- adjusting backrests;
- assisting residents to sit up in bed;
- adjusting bed height so that staff can provide care to the person, use moving and handling equipment at the bedside or make the bed without stooping or overreaching;
- helping the resident to stand up from sitting on the bed, as the bed can be adjusted to an appropriate height for the resident.

3.20 Training in the use of EPBs is necessary in order to maximise their benefits. This should include how to:

- operate and deactivate the bed controls and whether the beds are fitted with battery back-up (as disconnection from mains power may not be sufficient to prevent inadvertent operation);
- use the knee brace/break to prevent residents slipping down the bed;
- adjust the bed height when providing care or during handling tasks.

3.21 Although EPBs bring clear benefits, you should consider a number of issues when introducing them:

- They are significantly heavier than standard non-profiling beds and can potentially increase risks from moving them, especially on soft floor surfaces or where there are shallow inclines.
- Electric cables to beds can be damaged if the bed, or other mobile equipment, is moved while plugged in. Trailing cables can also cause a trip hazard.
- There is a risk of residents and visitors getting trapped in moving parts. Residents can be particularly vulnerable due to mental illness or confusion. Potential control measures include:
  - disabling foot controls so that the bed does not move if they are accidentally operated;
  - leaving the mattress platform in its lowest position when immobile residents are unattended;
  - locking-off some of the bed controls if appropriate.

Training

3.22 You are required to provide adequate information, instruction, training and supervision to ensure the health and safety of employees and others. Your assessments should identify what training and instruction is needed to ensure employees are competent in moving, handling and safe use of equipment.

3.23 The nature of some of the tasks and equipment mean the training will need to include practical instructions, demonstrations and practice, eg safe use of a hoist and sling, or coordinating a two-person handling task.

3.24 Monitoring should include checks that staff are using safe practices and should identify whether further instruction, training and/or supervision are required.

Key points to consider

- Have you assessed all hazardous moving and handling tasks carried out in the care home?
- Do you have person-centred moving and handling plans in place?
- Are plans specific about different handling tasks and the equipment to be used?
- Are plans reviewed periodically, and when the person's needs change, eg when they become less mobile and more dependent?
- Are staff competent to carry out moving and handling techniques safely?
- Is sufficient and appropriate moving and handling equipment available?
- Do your monitoring arrangements check that safe techniques and equipment are used, eg do you ensure that staff are using the right slings for the resident?

Find out more

HSE webpages on moving and handling in health and social care: www.hse.gov.uk/healthservices/moving-handling.htm

HSE's manual handling/MSDs website: www.hse.gov.uk/msd/manualhandling.htm

The Guide to the Handling of People: A Systems Approach (Sixth edition) Backcare 2011 ISBN 978 0 9530582 1 1 www.backcare.org.uk

National Back Exchange: www.nationalbackexchange.org

Chartered Society of Physiotherapists: www.csp.org.uk

The Disabled Living Foundation: www.dlf.org.uk

Medicines and Healthcare products Regulatory Agency (MHRA): www.mhra.gov.uk

Chapter 4 Equipment safety

4.1 Every year there are numerous accidents to employees and residents from using work equipment in social care. Many are serious and some are fatal. Ensuring that your staff are competent to do the job safely and use appropriate, well-maintained equipment can prevent accidents.

Key legislation

- Provision and Use of Work Equipment Regulations 1998 (PUWER)
- Lifting Operations and Lifting Equipment Regulations 1998 (LOLER)
- Electricity at Work Regulations 1989

Role of the Medicines and Healthcare products Regulatory Agency (MHRA)

4.2 MHRA has responsibility for ensuring that medicines and medical devices are effective and acceptably safe. You should be aware that MHRA asks healthcare workers, carers, patients and members of the public to report adverse incidents involving medical devices. When a medical device is suspected or known to be faulty, MHRA will work with manufacturers and distributors on the most appropriate and timely action to take.

What you need to do

Provision and Use of Work Equipment Regulations 1998 (PUWER)

4.3 Generally, any equipment used by an employee at work comes under the requirements of PUWER. This places duties on you as an employer and equipment providers, who own, operate or have control over work equipment. In a care home, this not only includes equipment used in kitchens, laundries, gardens and workshops – it can also include equipment provided for care, including bed rails, hoists, electric profiling beds, thermostatic mixing valves and medical equipment. Controlling the risks from the use of work equipment includes:

- proper installation;
- only using it for intended purposes;
- ensuring the work equipment is properly maintained (keeping a maintenance log where necessary);
- ensuring that people using, supervising or managing the equipment are provided with appropriate health and safety information (eg written instructions, or equipment markings) and receive adequate training;
- taking account of the working conditions and health and safety risks when selecting work equipment (eg flooring conditions, stairs, and space).

Lifting Operations and Lifting Equipment Regulations 1998 (LOLER)

4.4 LOLER places duties on you as an employer when your employees use lifting equipment. It also places duties on external equipment providers who retain ownership or control of the equipment. Essentially, LOLER requires that lifting equipment is:

- strong and stable enough for the particular use;
- marked to indicate safe working loads;

- positioned and installed to minimise any risks;
- maintained and visually checked before use – report obvious damage or wear;
- used safely, ie the work is planned, organised and performed by competent people;
- subject to thorough examination and inspection by competent people, where appropriate.

4.5 LOLER applies to equipment that lifts or lowers loads as a principal function. This includes passenger lifts hoists, bath lifts and slings. You can find more information in the HSE information sheet *How the Lifting Operations and Lifting Equipment Regulations apply to health and social care* (HSIS4), which lists common social care work equipment, and indicates whether LOLER applies – see 'Find out more' at the end of the chapter.

Marking of equipment and accessories

4.6 Lifting equipment and accessories, such as slings, should be uniquely identifiable. Manufacturers often label slings with a serial number, although these can fade over time, or during laundering. While it is fine to write on the label, be careful of using some permanent markers on the fabric and load-bearing webbing of slings because markers may contain solvents that can weaken the fabric. Attaching an identifying label (eg by using a robust cable tie) is acceptable, but labels should not be sewn onto the sling fabric as this can also weaken it. If in doubt, contact your supplier/manufacturer.

Thorough examination

4.7 Periodic thorough examination is required for lifting equipment exposed to conditions causing deterioration (such as wear, corrosion, damage etc) that could lead to fatal or serious injury.

4.8 The interval between periodic thorough examinations should be 6 months or less for lifting accessories and for equipment lifting people, and 12 months or less for other lifting equipment, or as specified in a dedicated scheme of examination. The dedicated scheme of examination may often specify periods that are different (longer or shorter) from the 'periodic' thorough examination intervals (ie 6 or 12 months). It should also be thoroughly examined each time exceptional circumstances, which are liable to jeopardise the safety of the lifting equipment, have occurred.

4.9 If lifting equipment requires thorough examination, you must do so before it is first used (unless you have written evidence that such an examination has already taken place). If lifting equipment requires thorough examination, you must have written evidence that this has been carried out before it is first used.

4.10 Where the safety of the equipment depends on the installation conditions (eg a tracked ceiling hoist), it must be thoroughly examined in situ before it is used, to ensure it is safe to operate.

4.11 A competent person should determine the thorough examination scheme. They should have enough practical and theoretical knowledge and experience of the lifting equipment to enable them to detect defects or weaknesses, and assess how important they are in relation to the safety and continued use of the equipment.

4.12 An in-house person may have sufficient expertise to examine simpler, lower-risk devices and accessories, but this should not generally be someone who also carries out routine maintenance (as they would be assessing their own work). Competent people should be able to act with impartiality and independence. The employer should consider independent verification of the in-house competent person's work.

4.13 You should keep records of thorough examinations and instruct staff to check that equipment is within date of examination before use. Some organisations also use colour-coded tags to indicate equipment is within its examination period.

Inspections
4.14 Lifting equipment and accessories may need to be inspected at suitable intervals between thorough examinations. This would normally include visual and functional checks where your risk assessment has identified a significant risk from use of the equipment, eg everyday wear and tear on slings. If inspections are required:

- the scope and frequency of inspection will depend on the opinion of the competent person and/or the manufacturer's instructions;
- the detail of the inspection needed should be included in any thorough examination scheme.

Routine maintenance
4.15 Routine maintenance typically involves checking and replacing worn or damaged parts, lubrication, and making routine adjustments. This is to ensure the equipment continues to operate as intended, and risks associated with wear or deterioration are avoided. Follow the manufacturer's guidance, especially where failure to do so might lead to harm.

Stair lifts and vertical lift platforms
4.16 If stair lifts are installed in your home, residents should be assessed to see whether they are able to use them safely without assistance. Where residents require help in using a stair lift, staff should be trained in its safe use and the best way to assist the resident. Stair lifts used in a care home should comply with ISO 9386:2000 and BS 81-40:2008.

4.17 Sometimes vertical lifting platforms are installed to help residents with impaired mobility bypass short flights of stairs. They should be manufactured to ISO 9386 Part 1: *Vertical lifting platforms* and advice on the design, construction, installation, operation and maintenance of vertical lifting platforms is provided in BS 6440:2011 *Powered vertical lifting platforms having non-enclosed or partially enclosed liftways intended for use by persons with impaired mobility – Specification*.

4.18 Following a number of serious incidents on vertical lifting platforms, if one is installed in your home, you should ensure that emergency override controls or keys are only used in the case of an emergency. They should not be used to allow continued use of lifting platforms where intermittent or ongoing faults are experienced.

Electrical safety

4.19 Electrical equipment and installations must be maintained to prevent danger. Poorly maintained electrical systems can cause electric shocks and fires.

Fixed electrical installations
4.20 The fixed electrical installation includes the incoming supply cables, switchgear, distribution boards, socket outlets etc. To reduce risks from the electrical installation, it is essential that it is properly installed and maintained.

4.21 The most widely used standard in the UK covering installation and maintenance is BS 7671:2008 (2013) *Requirements for electrical installations* (also known as the 17th Edition of the IET Wiring Regulations). BS 7671 is a code of practice that is widely recognised and accepted in the UK and compliance with it is likely to satisfy relevant requirements of the Electricity at Work Regulations 1989.

4.22 The Electricity at Work Regulations 1989 (EAWR) do not specify a frequency for maintenance. The legal requirement is simply to maintain the installation in a safe condition. Decisions on the frequency should be based on a risk assessment. However, the guidance notes supporting BS 7671 suggest that the fixed electrical installations in residential premises (including care homes) should be inspected and tested by a competent person every five years – although the interval can be varied on the advice of a competent person and the results of your risk assessment.

4.23 If visual checks are carried out, staff should be trained in what to look for (eg broken socket covers) but should be instructed not to dismantle or attempt to repair equipment unless they are competent to do so.

Portable electrical equipment

4.24 Portable equipment that can cause danger (including equipment owned by a resident) must be maintained. However, it is not a legal requirement to test all portable electrical appliances every year. You should decide the level and frequency of maintenance needed according to the risk of the item becoming faulty. The more often a piece of equipment is moved, the more likely it is to become damaged.

4.25 In deciding how often to maintain portable equipment you should consider:

- whether it is earthed or double insulated;
- if it is hand-held;
- its age;
- how often it is used;
- where it will be used.

4.26 In many cases a simple visual inspection by a member of staff who knows what to look for is enough (eg checking for loose cables, bare wires or signs of fire damage). However, in some cases, a portable appliance test may be required, eg in Class 1 earthed equipment such as floor cleaners and some kitchen/laundry equipment. More information on maintaining portable equipment can be found in HSE guidance (see 'Find out more' below).

Key points to consider

- Is work equipment adequately maintained in accordance with PUWER?
- Is lifting equipment (including accessories) being examined in accordance with LOLER?
- Is electrical equipment properly maintained?
- Have staff been trained in the safe use of equipment, and do you check that they are following their training?

Find out more

HSE webpage on equipment safety in health and social care: www.hse.gov.uk/healthservices/equipment-safety.htm

How the Lifting Operations and Lifting Equipment Regulations apply to health and social care HSIS4 (rev1) HSE 2012 www.hse.gov.uk/pubns/hsis4.htm

Safe use of work equipment. Provision and Use of Work Equipment Regulations 1998. Approved Code of Practice and guidance L22 (Third edition) HSE Books 2008 ISBN 978 0 7176 6295 1 www.hse.gov.uk/pubns/books/l22.htm

Safe use of lifting equipment. Lifting Operations and Lifting Equipment Regulations 1998. Approved Code of Practice and guidance L113 HSE Books 1998 ISBN 978 0 7176 1628 2 www.hse.gov.uk/pubns/books/l113.htm

Maintaining portable electric equipment in low-risk environments Leaflet INDG236(rev3) HSE Books 2013 www.hse.gov.uk/pubns/indg236.htm

Electrical safety and you: A brief guide Leaflet INDG231(rev1) HSE Books 2012 www.hse.gov.uk/pubns/indg231.htm

Medicines and Healthcare products Regulatory Agency (MHRA): www.mhra.gov.uk

ISO 9386:2000 Part 1: *Vertical lifting platforms* British Standards Institution

BS 81-40:2008 *Safety rules for the construction and installation of lifts. Special lifts for the transport of persons and goods. Stairlifts and inclined lifting platforms intended for persons with impaired mobility* British Standards Institution

BS 6440:2011 *Powered vertical lifting platforms having non-enclosed or partially enclosed liftways intended for use by persons with impaired mobility – Specification* British Standards Institution

BS 7671:2008 (2013) *Requirements for electrical installations* (also known as the 17th Edition of the IET Wiring Regulations) British Standards Institution

Chapter 5 Safe use of bed rails

5.1 Bed rails, also known as side rails or cot sides, are commonly used in care homes to reduce the risk of falls from beds. They can be a very effective means of preventing falls when used with the right bed, in the right way, for the right resident.

5.2 Poorly fitted bed rails have caused asphyxiation where a resident's neck, chest or limbs have become trapped in gaps between the bed rails, or between the bed rail and the bed, headboard or mattress. Other risks include rolling over the top of the rail, climbing over the rail, climbing over the footboard, violently shaking and dislodging rails and forceful contact with bed-rail parts.

Key legislation

- Provision and Use of Work Equipment Regulations 1998

5.3 Bed rails are considered as work equipment when used in care homes. They are also 'medical devices', so product safety issues such as their design and supply fall under the authority of the Medicines and Healthcare products Regulatory Agency (MHRA).

What you need to do

5.4 You should assess the risk of a resident falling from bed. The assessment should consider whether bed rails are the appropriate means of managing that risk. For example, if the individual is likely to try to climb over the rails due to confusion, then other control measures (such as extra-low beds and/or sensor alarms) will be more appropriate.

5.5 When considering the use of bed rails, you should bear in mind that they are not intended to:

- limit freedom of movement;
- restrain people;
- be used as grab handles.

5.6 Every effort should be made to involve the resident or their family in the decision-making process and to explain why and how bed rails are used. Families sometimes expect bed rails to be used out of concern for the safety of their relatives, not realising the potential risks, and that their use may not be the best approach.

5.7 Where bed rails are fitted, employees will need to be aware of the risks and how to ensure the resident's safety. Information on whether bed rails are used should be included in the resident's care plan.

Ensuring the correct use of bed rails

5.8 When using bed rails, consider the compatibility of the resident, bed, mattress, bed rail and any associated equipment. Both bed rails should be used to eliminate gaps between the bed and other furniture or wall and to help keep the mattress in position. Some key points to consider include the potential for entrapment:

- underneath the rail;
- between the end of the rail and the headboard or footboard;
- between the rail and the side of the mattress;
- between the bed-rail bars.

Entrapment underneath the rail

5.9 The resident can become trapped between the bottom of the rail and the mattress if the gap beneath the rail is too large. This could be due to:

- incompatibility of bed rail and bed;
- using an airflow mattress in conjunction with a thin-base mattress;
- using easily compressible base mattresses or a mattress which is too small for the bed.

5.10 Using an airflow mattress, which may be more compressible at the edges, in conjunction with thinner or easily compressible base mattresses, could allow access to the gap under the rail. Entrapment under the rail can result in asphyxiation (see Figure 1).

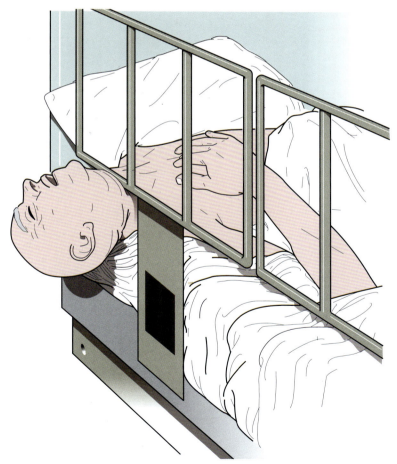

Figure 1 Entrapment under the rail can lead to asphyxiation

5.11 British Standard BS EN 60601-2-52:2010 states that the gap from any accessible opening between the bottom of the side rail and the mattress platform should be no more than 60 mm. When assessing this gap, you should take into consideration whether mattresses are thin, easily compressible at the edge and whether the individual's dimensions increase the risk of slipping underneath the rails. In addition, mattresses should always fit snugly, with no significant gap, between both bed rails.

[Note: BS EN 60601-2-52:2010 came into force for all new equipment manufactured or supplied from 1 April 2013.]

Entrapment between the end of the rail and the headboard or footboard

5.12 Residents can become trapped between the end of the bed rail and the headboard or footboard if the rails are not secured in a safe position.

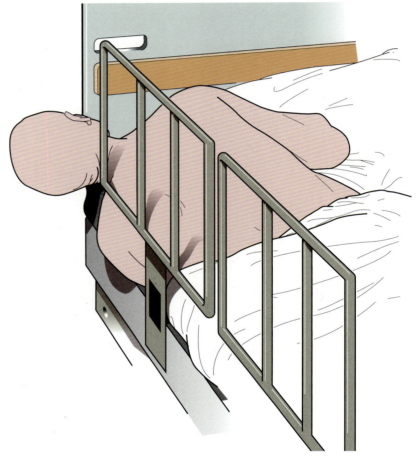

Figure 2 Entrapment between the end of the bed rail and the headboard

5.13 British Standard BS EN 60601-2-52:2010 states that:

- the gap between the end of the bed rail and headboard should be no more than 60 mm;
- the gap between the footboard and end of the bed rail should either be 60 mm or less, or greater than 318 mm, to prevent asphyxiation;
- likewise, where two-section split rails are used, the gap between the two sections should be 60 mm or less, or greater than 318 mm.

Entrapment between the bed rail and the side of the mattress

5.14 Entrapment in the space between the side of the mattress and the rail can be caused by:

- a poorly fitting mattress;
- poorly fitting bed rail system and/or insecure fittings that allow the bed rail to move away from the side of the bed;
- bed rails only being used on one side of the bed, allowing the mattress to move away from it.

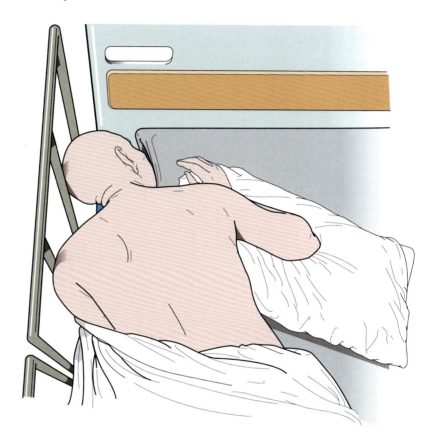

Figure 3 Entrapment between the bed rail and the side of the mattress

5.15 Replacement mattresses that are narrower than the original mattress, or smaller speciality mattresses used on top of existing mattresses, may result in an excessive gap between the mattress and the bed rail. Poorly maintained bed rails may be too flexible, may deform under force or have too much play in their fixings, resulting in a gap between the mattress edge and rail.

5.16 The mattress should fit snugly between both rails so it does not allow entrapment of the occupant's head or body. You should check this gap, taking into account the resident using the bed rails. If you require further advice, contact your bed rail supplier – they should be able to carry out the tests detailed in the British Standard. Accessories such as bed-rail bumpers or gap fillers can be used in conjunction with bed rails. If used (in conjunction with a correctly fitted bed rail), accessories should be robust, so they cannot accidentally be displaced or easily damaged.

Risk of falls when using bed rails

5.17 Falls can occur if a resident climbs or rolls over the top of the rails. The height of a bed rail above the level of the compressed mattress can prevent an inadvertent fall from a bed. BS EN 60601-2-52:2010 quotes a minimum height of 220 mm, measured vertically from the top edge of an uncompressed mattress to the top of the bed rail.

5.18 Replacing a mattress with one significantly thicker than that intended by the bed manufacturer, placing one mattress on top of another, or using mattress overlays or airflow mattresses, may reduce the effectiveness of the bed rails because the relative height of the rail is reduced. This could increase the risk of a person involuntarily rolling or falling over the top of the bed rail. Care providers should check whether the bed rails are high enough to take into account any increase in mattress thickness or additional overlay.

5.19 BS EN 60601-2-52:2010 states that, where a 'speciality' or 'mattress overlay' is used and the side rail does not meet the minimum height of 220 mm above the mattress, a risk assessment should be carried out to assure equivalent safety.

Key points to consider

- Are bed rails only provided where they are the most appropriate solution to prevent falls?
- Are staff trained in the risks and safe use of bed rails?
- Are rails and any accessories compatible with the bed, mattress and occupant?
- Does the mattress fit snugly between the rails?
- Are rails correctly fitted on both sides of the bed, secure, regularly inspected and maintained?
- Are checks completed to ensure that gaps that could cause entrapment of neck, head, and chest are eliminated?

Find out more

HSE webpage on safe use of bed rails:
www.hse.gov.uk/healthservices/bed-rails.htm

BS EN 60601-2-52:2010 *Particular requirements for basic safety and essential performance of medical beds* British Standards Institution

Medicines and Healthcare products Regulatory Agency (MHRA) website: www.mhra.gov.uk (Includes the MHRA Device Bulletin DB 2006(06) v2.0 *Safe use of bed rails* November 2012)

Chapter 6 Slips, trips and falls on the level

6.1 Slips, trips and falls can have a serious impact on the lives of employees and they can also impact on those being cared for. People who live in care homes can be particularly vulnerable to injuries from falls. See Chapter 7 for advice on falls from height.

6.2 Many factors can cause slips and trips. The practical measures needed will vary in different situations. Some of the main causes of slips and trips accidents include:

- slippery or wet surfaces caused by water and/or other fluids;
- slippery surfaces caused by dry or dusty floor contamination such as lint or talcum powder;
- obstructions, both temporary and permanent;
- trip hazards, uneven surfaces and changes of level, eg unmarked ramps;
- poor levels of lighting.

Key legislation

- Workplace (Health, Safety and Welfare) Regulations 1992
- Management of Health and Safety at Work Regulations 1999

What you need to do

Controlling the risk

Residents
6.3 You should identify any individuals who are at particular risk and then put suitable and adequate control measures in place. Factors to consider include the following:

- *Age-related physiological changes* – age can increase the risk of falls, ie deteriorating vision, impaired judgement and memory, altered mobility and increased frailty and dependence. Falls may arise from weight shifting, trips or stumbles.
- *Medical conditions* – certain conditions may increase the risk of falls, ie strokes, dementia, fits and faints, low blood pressure, and urinary infections.
- *Medication* – certain medications may increase the risk of falling. Older people may have increased sensitivity to medications such as psychotropic drugs, sedatives, analgesics, beta-blockers, antidepressants, diuretics and antihypertensive drugs, which can all cause particular problems.

Employees
6.4 When assessing the risk to employees, you should:

- look at how work is organised and managed, eg to avoid rushing, overcrowding, trailing cables;
- consult employees on measures to control risks, eg when choosing the most appropriate protective footwear or when there is a proposed change in cleaning methods.

Environmental factors

Floors
6.5 Slip-resistant flooring should be used in bathrooms, kitchens or where surface contamination cannot be effectively controlled. Change in floor surface, eg stepping from carpet to a smooth floor or vice versa, can cause stumbles and slips, especially for people with impaired vision or mobility. Where floor levels change, they should be clearly identified and hand rails should be considered. It should be noted that highly reflective materials may be a barrier for people with dementia. This may sometimes be a desired outcome if it helps to ensure their safety.

Contamination
6.6 Contamination can include food, liquids, urine, talcum powder, leaves and dirt from outside, and cleaning substances etc. Consider how you can prevent floors getting contaminated so far as reasonably practicable. Design tasks to minimise spillages and, if they cannot be prevented, control the contamination, eg by containing and effective cleaning.

Obstacles
6.7 Floors should be kept free from trip hazards and obstructions, eg avoid trailing wires and ensure equipment is stored away when not in use, rather than left in walkways.

Organisational factors

Cleaning
6.8 Decide how, when and how often floors should be cleaned and how spillages can be quickly and effectively dealt with. You need to decide on the most effective cleaning method and avoid introducing more slip or trip risks. For example, smooth floors left damp by a mop are likely to be extremely slippery and access to these areas should be restricted until they are dry. Spillages or localised contamination should be spot cleaned to reduce the risk of widening the contaminated area. Where traditional mopping takes place, there should be adequate segregation until the floor is dry. Effective training and supervision is essential.

Footwear
6.9 Where your risk assessment shows there is a risk of slips and trip injuries, consider providing staff with suitable footwear for the environment or work activity. For example, where floors are likely to be contaminated (eg food preparation or wet rooms), staff may require slip-resistant footwear. Cleaners are likely to be exposed to wet floors on a regular basis and appropriate footwear should be provided.
It may be appropriate to advise residents about suitable footwear, depending on individual factors.

Human factors
6.10 Have a positive attitude towards health and safety – a 'see it, sort it' mentality can reduce the risk of slips and trips accidents, eg dealing with a spillage, instead of waiting for someone else to do it.

Key points to consider

- Have you assessed the risks and put control measures in place?
- Is the flooring in different parts of your premises suitable for the activities carried out there (eg non-slip flooring in potential wet areas)?
- Do your floor cleaning methods create additional slip risks (eg leaving the floor wet at a time/place where residents might have access)?

- Are arrangements in place to ensure that floor surfaces are adequately maintained and free from trip hazards?
- Where residents are assessed as being at high risk of slips, trips and falls, are individual factors (taking the environment into account) included in the care plan, and are measures to reduce the risk in place?

Find out more

HSE's webpage on slips and trips in health and social care: www.hse.gov.uk/healthservices/slips

HSE's slips and trips website: www.hse.gov.uk/slips

Preventing slips and trips at work: A brief guide Leaflet INDG225(rev2) HSE Books 2012 www.hse.gov.uk/pubns/indg225.htm

Designing interiors for people with dementia University of Stirling www.dementiashop.co.uk

Chapter 7 Falls from height

7.1 Resident falls from windows, balconies or stairs can result in serious or fatal injuries and continue to be a serious issue. There are three broad categories of falls:

- *Accidental falls* – These can occur where a person is sitting on a window sill, leaning out or a window, or where the sill or banister height is low and acts as a pivot, allowing them to fall.
- *Falls arising out of confused mental state* – Many reported accidents involve residents in either a temporary or permanent confused mental state, often caused by senility or dementia, reduced mental capacity, mental disorder, or alcohol and drugs (both prescribed and illegal). In some cases, individuals try to escape from an environment they perceive to be hostile, and may use a window believing it to be an exit. Other factors may include unfamiliarity with new surroundings, uncomfortable temperatures, broken sleep and medication effects.
- *Deliberate self-harm* – This is a recognised risk for residents with certain mental health conditions.

7.2 Falls may occur when your employees (see paragraphs 7.10 to 7.12) or contractors carry out a number of maintenance activities, including window and gutter cleaning, minor roof repairs, and internal decorating. You should have effective arrangements in place to assess and manage the risks. The Workplace (Health, Safety and Welfare) Regulations 1992 referred to in this chapter only apply to employees, but standards applied will help to reduce risks to residents as well.

Key legislation

- Work at Height Regulations 2005
- Management of Health and Safety at Work Regulations 1999
- Workplace (Health, Safety and Welfare) Regulations 1992

What you need to do

Controlling the risks to residents

7.3 To adequately manage the risk of falls to residents, you need to assess the risks arising from the premises and any additional risks for individual residents. Where residents are at risk, further measures may be needed to prevent them falling from height.

Windows
7.4 Windows that can be fully opened and are accessible to people at risk of falling or climbing out must meet appropriate standards (see below). In assessing the risks, you should consider furniture, or other items, that may enable residents to climb over barriers, or access windows, which might otherwise be inaccessible. Where necessary, you should provide adequate cooling, eg high-level and/or restricted aperture ventilation, fans or air conditioning where window openings have been restricted.

7.5 Suitable controls may include the following:

- *Window restrictors* – Where vulnerable residents have access to window openings large enough to fall through, and at a height that could cause harm (eg above ground level), those windows should be restrained sufficiently to prevent such falls. Window restrictors should:

- restrict the window opening to 100 mm or less;
- be suitably robust to withstand foreseeable force applied by an individual determined to open the window further. Where the casement might distort, restrictors should be fitted at both sides of the window;
- be sufficiently robust to withstand damage (either deliberate or from general wear);
- be robustly secured using tamper-proof fittings so they cannot be removed or disengaged using readily accessible implements (such as cutlery). They should require a special tool or key for removal. Windows fitted with initial opening restrictors are not suitable in social care premises where individuals are at risk, as they can be easily overridden.

- *Window design* – The window frames and associated fittings must be sufficiently robust. The Workplace (Health, Safety and Welfare) Regulations 1992 Approved Code of Practice (Workplace ACOP) – and Building Regulations – require that the bottom edge of opening windows should normally be at least 800 mm above floor level, unless there is a barrier to prevent falls. This will reduce the risk of inadvertent falls where fully openable windows are assessed as being appropriate. See 'Find out more' at the end of the chapter for more details about the Workplace ACOP and Building Regulations.

Balconies

7.6 Where residents are at risk of falling, sufficient protection should be provided to prevent them from accessing balconies and external fire stairs, or climbing over the balcony edge protection. Take into account furniture or features with footholds, which may allow access over the rail/barrier (eg chairs, tables, plant pots and walls).

Stairs

7.7 Stairs can present a hazard to everyone, but there are a number of factors that are particularly relevant to residents and should be considered in the care plan. See also Chapter 6, paragraph 6.3.

7.8 Stairs should be in a safe condition, kept free of obstructions and well lit. If residents lack mobility and require extra support, then the stairs should have suitable hand rails on both sides. Ideally, stairs should not be steep, winding, curved, or have open risers.

7.9 It may be appropriate to restrict access to some stairs, eg steep cellar stairs or upper floor levels where residents are at risk of falls. Discuss this with a fire safety officer if it impacts on fire evacuation. You may also need to seek advice on how to prevent access through external fire doors so they can be released and quickly accessed in the event of a fire.

Controlling the risks to employees

Working at height

7.10 Before working at height you must work through these simple steps:

- avoid work at height where it is reasonably practicable to do so;
- where work at height cannot be avoided, prevent falls using either an existing place of work that is already safe or the right type of equipment;
- minimise the distance and consequences of a fall, by using the right type of equipment where the risk cannot be eliminated.

7.11 You should:

- do as much work as possible from the ground;
- ensure workers can get safely to and from where they work at height;
- ensure equipment is suitable, stable and strong enough for the job, maintained and checked regularly;
- make sure you don't overload or overreach when working at height;
- take precautions when working on or near fragile surfaces;
- provide protection from falling objects;
- consider your emergency evacuation and rescue procedures.

7.12 If a ladder is the right piece of equipment for these activities you should ensure it is the right type, and that it is checked, in a safe condition, and used safely. Where safety fixtures and fittings are installed, you must ensure they are functioning effectively and have not deteriorated as a result of use, wear or tampering.

7.13 If you are using a contractor to do work at height you must ensure they are doing the work safely and are not putting others at risk, eg taking safe access into account and providing protection from falling objects.

Key points to consider

- Are any of your residents at increased risk of falls from windows, balconies or other areas?
- If so, are the controls adequate, suitably robust and properly maintained?
- Where employees are working at height, are activities properly planned and organised?
- Is access equipment used for working at height suitable, maintained and inspected?
- Are employees trained and competent to do the work?

Find out more

Resident safety

HSE's webpage on falls from windows:
www.hse.gov.uk/healthservices/falls-windows.htm

Health Building Note 00-10 Part D: *Windows and associated hardware* Department of Health www.dhsspsni.gov.uk/hbn00-01-partd.pdf

Scottish Health Technical Memorandum (SHTM) 55: *Windows*
www.hfs.scot.nhs.uk/publications/shtm-55.pdf

Welsh Health Technical Memoranda HTM 55 Wales: *Windows*
www.wales.nhs.uk/sites3/docmetadata.cfm?orgid=254&id=202017

Fire safety risk assessment for residential care premises
Department for Communities and Local Government
www.communities.gov.uk/publications/fire/firesafetyrisk5

Practical Fire Safety Guidance for Care Homes Safer Scotland 2008
www.scotland.gov.uk/Resource/0040/00402331.pdf

Designing interiors for people with dementia University of Stirling
www.dementiashop.co.uk

Managing falls and fractures in care homes for older people: Good practice self-assessment resource Care Inspectorate Scotland www.careinspectorate.com

Employee safety

HSE's working at height website: www.hse.gov.uk/work-at-height

Working at height: A brief guide Leaflet INDG401(rev2) HSE Books 2014
www.hse.gov.uk/pubns/indg401.htm

Safe use of ladders and stepladders: A brief guide Leaflet INDG455
HSE Books 2014 www.hse.gov.uk/pubns/indg455.htm

Workplace health, safety and welfare. Workplace (Health, Safety and Welfare) Regulations 1992. Approved Code of Practice and guidance L24 (Second edition) HSE Books 2013 ISBN 978 0 7176 6583 9 www.hse.gov.uk/pubns/books/l24.htm

Building Regulations
Building Act 1984 (England and Wales): www.legislation.gov.uk/ukpga/1984/55
Building (Scotland) Act: www.legislation.gov.uk/asp/2003/8/contents

Approved Documents for Building Regulations in England and Wales:
www.planningportal.gov.uk/buildingregulations

Approved Documents for Building Regulations in Scotland:
www.scotland.gov.uk/Topics/Built-Environment/Building/Building-standards

Chapter 8 Hazardous substances, infections and diseases

8.1 Hazardous substances found in care homes include drugs and medicines, cleaning materials, disinfectants and maintenance products containing chemicals (eg pesticides). Infections and diseases can be caused by micro-organisms (eg those associated with soiled laundry or exposure to body fluids).

Key legislation

- Control of Substances Hazardous to Health Regulations 2002 (COSHH)
- Health and Safety (Sharps Instruments in Healthcare) Regulations 2013

What you need to do

8.2 You must assess the health risk to your staff, residents and visitors, and decide on the action you need to take to prevent or control exposure to hazardous substances, infections and diseases.

8.3 COSHH assessments should be relatively simple in a care home. You should:

- establish what substances (eg cleaning agents) and biological hazards (eg hazardous waste or soiled laundry) are present and how they can cause harm;
- prevent exposure to hazardous substances by elimination where reasonably practicable. If this cannot be done;
  - decide whether you can substitute it for something safer, eg swap an irritant cleaning product for something milder;
  - if substitution is not possible, reduce the potential for exposure by ensuring you have safe systems for handling the substance following manufacturer instructions, and by securely storing products (eg cleaning products), keeping them in their original containers, and providing the right personal protective equipment (PPE).

8.4 Product hazard warnings may be found on labels, which for hazardous substances may include risk phrases such as 'avoid contact with skin'. If the information is not readily available on the label or an advisory leaflet, then obtain a data sheet for that product from the supplier or manufacturer. By law, your supplier must give you an up-to-date safety data sheet for a substance that is 'dangerous for supply'.

8.5 PPE should be provided if it is not reasonably practicable to prevent or otherwise control the risk. It should be suitable for the product and task as per the product instructions. Toilet cleaning chemicals may only require the use of rubber gloves, whereas caustic descalers and oven cleaners may require heavy-duty gloves, goggles or face shields and a well-ventilated area while the products are being used. Many of the risks for hazardous substances used in a care home can be grouped together when considering suitable control measures.

8.6 Employees must be given information, instruction and training on how to use and store the product safely, how to clear up spillages, and how to check and wear protective equipment correctly.

8.7 To help manage the risks to staff from some of the hazardous substances you may require specialist occupational health advice, eg health surveillance for skin problems caused by latex or wet work. Further information on occupational health can be found in Chapter 1 (paragraph 1.9).

Specific hazardous substances, infections and diseases

Skin irritants

8.8 Skin problems can be caused by frequent exposure to soaps and cleaners, and 'wet work'. Wet work involves wet hands or hand washing and, as a guideline, an employee is at risk of developing skin problems if they wash their hands more than 20 times a day. Other hazardous agents include rubber chemicals, which may be present in natural rubber latex and synthetic rubber materials, bleach and sterilisers, preservatives, and fragrances. The common skin problems include:

- *Dermatitis* – This is the most common form of work-related skin disease suffered by social care professionals. Dermatitis is an inflammatory condition of the skin caused by contact with outside agents, which can result in irritation, redness, cracking and blistering.
- *Urticaria* – This condition is caused by contact with something that irritates the skin or causes an allergic reaction. Contact urticaria is different from dermatitis. In particular, it usually occurs quickly following skin contact and disappears again within hours. Common causes of urticaria are latex protein in single-use latex gloves, some foods (eg potatoes, fish, meat), and cold or heat.
- *Latex allergies* – Natural rubber latex (NRL) proteins have the potential to cause dermatitis.

[Note: More serious allergic reactions, such as anaphylaxis, are also possible. The proteins naturally present in NRL cause the allergies through direct contact with the skin.]

8.9 You should put in place suitable control measures to manage the risks. Employees should be advised to:

- avoid direct contact between unprotected hands and substances, products and wet work where this is sensible and practical;
- protect the skin – avoiding contact will not always be possible;
- check their hands regularly for the first signs of itchy, dry or red skin. If they suspect problems they should seek advice from a medical practitioner or occupational health service.

Selecting gloves

8.10 You should carefully consider the risks when selecting gloves because of the significance of latex gloves as a source of exposure to NRL proteins. In summary, HSE's glove selection guidance (latex or otherwise) is as follows:

- Decide if protective gloves are required at all to perform the task.
- If protective gloves are needed, they must be suitable for the task being carried out.

8.11 If your assessment leads to latex as the most suitable glove type for protection against the hazard, then:

- single-use latex gloves should be low-protein and powder-free;
- people with existing allergy to NRL proteins should take latex avoidance measures and should not use single-use or reusable latex gloves. Employers may therefore need to provide gloves of an alternative material;

- where the use of gloves may result in direct or indirect exposure to members of the public, you must assess the risks of such exposure and adopt suitable control measures to ensure the health of others is protected.

Infection prevention and control

8.12 Control of infection is an important consideration throughout the care home environment. There may be the potential for exposure to a range of human pathogens with the resulting risk of harm or disease. All care homes should have an infection prevention and control policy that addresses such issues as:

- education and training of employees in infection prevention and control issues, including outbreaks of infection;
- protocols for hand washing;
- service user isolation/placement;
- aseptic procedures;
- good sanitation – disinfection and decontamination, including domestic cleaning;
- ill-health reporting and recording;
- monitoring, surveillance and audit;
- prevention of exposure to blood-borne viruses, including prevention of sharps injuries and immunisation policies for at-risk staff;
- use of PPE, including gloves;
- creation, collection and disposal of clinical waste.

Risks from blood and body fluids

8.13 Employees working in care homes, particularly nurses, are sometimes at risk from infections carried in blood and body fluids, including hepatitis B, C and human immunodeficiency virus (HIV). If there is a risk of becoming infected due to work activities, you need to assess these risks to decide upon suitable controls.

8.14 General precautions include covering cuts/grazes with waterproof dressings, good personal hygiene, good environmental hygiene, cleaning and disinfecting contaminated equipment, and wearing single-use gloves and disposable aprons for high-risk/messy activities.

8.15 A 'sharps injury' is an incident involving a needle or sharp instrument penetrating the skin. If the sharp is contaminated with blood or other body fluid, there is a potential for infection. If there is a risk from sharps injuries, precautions include:

- where possible, eliminate the use of sharps devices;
- if this is not possible, replace conventional devices, where reasonably practicable, with safer sharps devices – incorporating features or mechanisms to prevent or minimise the risk of injury, eg syringes and needles are now available with a shield or cover that slides or pivots to cover the needle after use;
- ensuring needles are not resheathed after use, but are disposed of directly into a sharps container;
- ensuring that suitable clinical waste disposal procedures are followed, including use of sharps containers;
- ensuring all employees, and workers under your control, have information and instruction on safe use of sharps;
- providing access to occupational health advice, and immunisation, where appropriate;
- having clear procedures for responding to sharps injuries, including speedy access to appropriate prophylaxis treatments.

8.16 Employees should have clear instructions on how to safely clear up and disinfect a spillage of infected blood/body fluids. You should specify the safety measures that employees should take, such as how much ventilation is required and what PPE should be worn. It is often useful to have such a procedure written down and kept with the spillage kit/chemicals for disinfecting blood/body fluid spills.

8.17 In care homes where there is known to be a high incidence of hepatitis B among residents, you should offer employees appropriate immunisation. You should have an agreed arrangement with an occupational health service (see pararaph 1.9) or a GP for the immunisation of employees. Once employees have been immunised, periodic checks to ensure that they remain adequately protected by the vaccine will be needed. Employees cannot be charged for vaccines.

Hazardous waste

8.18 Employees may have to deal with waste that is potentially hazardous to the handler, residents, and others. In general, the majority of waste in care homes falls under the category of 'offensive/hygiene' waste. This is waste which is non-infectious and which does not require specialist treatment or disposal, but which may be offensive for those coming into contact with it. Hazardous waste would be generated when infection is known or suspected.

8.19 Sharps waste follows special or hazardous waste streams, depending on items used and what they have been used for. Hazardous drugs will also require special attention and the waste streams used may vary between the different countries of Great Britain. Where any doubt exists, you should seek advice from the local Environment Agency office or local authority.

8.20 All employees who are required to handle and move hazardous waste should be adequately trained in safe procedures on how to deal with spillages or other incidents. Refresher training may also be required. It is also advisable to keep training records.

8.21 Spillage kits are recommended. These should contain disposable aprons, single-use gloves, clinical waste bags and tags, paper towels, sodium hypochlorite and instructions to help ensure employees take the correct action.

8.22 Hazardous waste containers should be stored in an appropriate place until they are removed from the care home. They should not be allowed to accumulate in corridors or other places accessible to residents or members of the public. The area where the waste is stored should be designated for hazardous waste, and be enclosed and secure.

8.23 Safe disposal of hazardous waste is the responsibility of the care provider. Transfer notes or other documentation help to establish that hazardous waste has been disposed of correctly. The domestic waste collection service should not be used for hazardous waste.

Medicines and drugs

8.24 Certain medicines are 'hazardous' and may cause significant risk if there is direct occupational exposure – in their intact state (eg as a tablet or capsule), or if they are crushed or dissolved, or if a capsule is opened. However, no medicine is completely risk-free and they may affect different people in different ways, so appropriate precautions must be taken when handling all types of medicines.

8.25 Some medicines have specific storage requirements to preserve their effectiveness and potency. In some cases, the expiry date of drugs is shortened if medicines are taken out of their original containers or stored in different conditions, eg insulin will store until the manufacturers' expiry date if stored between 2 °C and 8 °C but only for 28–30 days at room temperature.

8.26 Medicines should be kept secure, locked away and free from heat, moisture and light. Seek advice on all these issues from a pharmacist and follow their instructions to ensure safe management and administration of the drugs. In addition, the patient information leaflets provide information on storage and handling.

8.27 Hazardous drugs – including cytotoxic drugs used for chemotherapy, some hormones and antiviral drugs – can cause adverse health effects to the person administering the medicine if they are inadvertently exposed. Other drugs and medicines can be dangerous if misused, or if accidentally taken.

8.28 When a care home looks after a person's medication, the registered manager/ provider is responsible for the safe and appropriate handling of those medicines. You must ensure you have written policies, procedures and guidelines in place to manage all aspects of medication handling and that these policies are monitored and reviewed.

Key points to consider

- Have you assessed the risks to staff and others from exposure to hazardous substances?
- Have you introduced appropriate precautions to prevent or control the risk?
- Do you inform, instruct and train staff about the risks and precautions to be taken?
- Are staff given appropriate protective equipment/clothing?
- Do you ensure that the precautions are used, and procedures followed?
- Are hazardous substances safely stored, eg locked in a cupboard and out of reach of vulnerable adults?

Find out more

HSE's health and social care website: www.hse.gov.uk/healthservices

COSHH

A step by step guide to COSHH assessment HSG97 (Second edition) HSE Books 2004 ISBN 978 0 7176 2785 1 www.hse.gov.uk/pubns/books/hsg97.htm

Control of substances hazardous to health (COSHH). The Control of Substances Hazardous to Health Regulations 2002 (as amended). Approved Code of Practice and guidance L5 (Sixth edition) HSE Books 2013 ISBN 978 0 7176 6582 2 www.hse.gov.uk/pubns/books/l5.htm

Working with substances hazardous to health: A brief guide to COSHH Leaflet INDG136(rev5) HSE Books 2012 www.hse.gov.uk/pubns/indg136.htm

Skin

HSE's skin at work website: www.hse.gov.uk/skin

Infection prevention and control

HSE's infections at work website: www.hse.gov.uk/biosafety/infection.htm

Health and Safety (Sharp Instruments in Healthcare) Regulations 2013: Guidance for employers and employees Health Services Information Sheet HSIS7 HSE 2013 www.hse.gov.uk/pubns/hsis7.htm

New and expectant mothers who work: A brief guide to your health and safety Leaflet INDG373(rev2) HSE Books 2013 www.hse.gov.uk/pubns/indg373.htm

Prevention and control of infection in care homes: An information resource Department of Health/Public Health England
www.gov.uk/government/publications

Hazardous waste

Health Technical Memorandum 07-01 *Safe management of healthcare waste* Department of Health
www.gov.uk/government/publications

SEPA guidance on clinical waste:
www.sepa.org.uk/waste/waste_regulation/clinical_waste.aspx

Drugs and medicines

Care home staff – a one-stop resource for care home staff MHRA:
www.mhra.gov.uk/safetyinformation/Healthcareproviders/Carehomestaff

Royal Pharmaceutical Society of Great Britain: www.rpharms.com

Chapter 9 Legionella

9.1 Legionnaires' disease is a potentially fatal form of pneumonia. It is normally contracted by inhaling tiny, airborne droplets containing viable legionella bacteria. Although everyone is susceptible to infection, the risk increases with age and some people are at a higher risk, such as people over 45, smokers, heavy drinkers, people suffering from chronic respiratory or kidney disease, diabetes, lung and heart disease and anyone with an impaired immune system. Water systems in care homes, with residents likely to be particularly vulnerable, need particular consideration.

9.2 Although legionella bacteria are widespread in natural water sources, outbreaks of the illness occur from exposure to legionella growing in purpose-built systems where water is maintained at a temperature high enough to encourage growth (between 20–45 °C) and where there are nutrients that support bacterial growth such as rust, sludge, scale, organic matter and biofilms. The bacteria are dormant below 20 °C and do not survive above 60 °C. Airborne water droplets are created by water systems such as hot and cold water services, atomisers, wet air-conditioning plant, spa baths and hydrotherapy baths.

9.3 When managing water temperatures to control legionella in care homes, you should consider potential scald risks – see Chapter 10.

Key legislation

- Control of Substances Hazardous to Health Regulations (COSHH) 2002 – see 'Find out more' at the end of this chapter for details of the relevant Approved Code of Practice (ACOP) for those Regulations and also the ACOP on legionnaires' disease

What you need to do

9.4 A competent person, who understands the water systems and any equipment associated with it, should assess the risks of your hot and cold water systems, and advise on whether adequate measures are in place to control the risk of exposure to legionella bacteria. To achieve this, you may need to develop a simplified but accurate illustration of the layout of the water system, ie a schematic diagram.

9.5 The traditional strategy for reducing and controlling the risk from legionella is water temperature control. Water services should be operated at temperatures that prevent legionella growth:

- hot water storage cylinders (calorifiers) should store water at 60 °C or higher;
- hot water should be distributed at 50 °C or higher (thermostatic mixing valves may be required where scald risk is identified – see Chapter 10);
- cold water should be maintained, where possible, below 20 °C.

9.6 A competent person should routinely check, inspect and clean the system, in accordance with the risk assessment and as set out in HSE's ACOP *Legionnaires' disease* (L8) and the guide *Legionnaires' disease: Control of legionella* (HSG274) Part 2: 'Hot and cold water systems' (see the paragraphs below and 'Find out more' at the end of the chapter). The frequency for inspecting and monitoring the hot and cold water systems will depend on their complexity and the susceptibility of those using the water. Table 2 provides a checklist with an indication of frequency for inspection and monitoring.

Table 2 Management of legionella (example checklist): hot and cold water services

Service	Task	Frequency
Hot water services	Inspect calorifier internally and clean by draining the vessel. Frequency should be subject to the findings and increased or decreased based on conditions recorded Where there is no inspection hatch, purge any debris in the base to a suitable drain, collect the initial flush from the base to inspect clarity, quantity of debris and temperature	Annually, or as indicated by rate of fouling
	Check flow and return temperatures at calorifiers are at least 60 °C and 50 °C respectively	Monthly
	Check the water has reached 50 °C after running it for up to one minute at the sentinel outlets (furthest and closest to each tank or cylinder)	Monthly
	Take temperatures at a representative selection of other outlets to create a temperature profile of the whole system over a defined time period	Representative selection considered on a rotational basis to ensure the whole system is reaching satisfactory temperatures for legionella control
Cold water services	Check tank water temperatures remote from ball valve and incoming mains. Record maximum temperatures of the stored and supply water	Annually (summer) or as indicated by the temperature profiling
	Check the water is below 20 °C within two minutes of running the cold tap	Monthly
	Visually inspect cold water storage tanks and carry out remedial work where necessary	Annually
	Take temperatures at a representative selection of other outlets to confirm they are below 20 °C to create a temperature profile of the whole system over a defined time period	Representative selection considered on a rotational basis to ensure the whole system is reaching satisfactory temperatures for legionella control
Shower heads	Dismantle, clean and descale removable parts, shower heads, inserts and hoses, where fitted	Quarterly, or as indicated by the rate of fouling or other risk factors
Infrequently used outlets	Where possible, remove infrequently used outlets. Otherwise, flush through until temperature stabilises and purge to drain	Weekly, or as indicated by the risk assessment
Bacterial analysis	If considered necessary by the risk assessment, samples should be carried out in accordance with BS 7592:2008 and analysed by a UKAS-accredited laboratory	Periodically (as identified through risk assessment)

9.7 Sentinel points (typically the taps furthest and closest to each tank or cylinder) should be identified and checked monthly for the distribution temperatures. Hot water should reach at least 50 °C within one minute of running the outlet. Cold water should be below 20 °C within two minutes. You should also check the hot water storage cylinder temperatures every month. Cold water tank incoming mains temperature should be checked annually; this should be done in the summer. Where the hot water circulates, the outgoing temperature should measure at least 60 °C and return water at least 50 °C. You should keep a record of the checks/temperatures.

9.8 Stagnant water supports legionella growth. To reduce the risk, you should:

- remove dead legs/dead ends in pipework;
- flush out infrequently used outlets (including shower heads and taps) at least weekly (or remove where possible);
- clean and descale shower heads and hoses at least quarterly or in accordance with manufacturers' instructions.

9.9 Cold water storage tanks should be inspected annually to check the condition inside and outside, and the water in them, and any cleaning or remedial work carried out where necessary. Water should be drained from hot water cylinders to check for debris or signs of corrosion.

9.10 Where monitoring for legionella is considered appropriate in hot and cold water systems, eg where temperatures are not being consistently achieved throughout the system or the effectiveness of any control regime is in doubt, it should be carried out in accordance with BS 7592:2008. HSE's guidance *Legionnaires' disease: Control of legionella* (HSG274, Part 2) provides further information – see 'Find out more' below.

9.11 Where refurbishment, extensions or new buildings are planned, systems should be designed to minimise legionella growth, by:

- keeping pipework as short and direct as possible;
- adequately insulating pipes and tanks;
- using materials that do not encourage the growth of legionella;
- preventing contamination, eg by fitting tanks with lids and insect screens.

9.12 Other control methods, when used correctly and properly managed, can be effective to control legionella, eg chlorine dioxide or copper/silver ionisation. To ensure they remain effective, their application will need suitable assessment and require meticulous control as part of the overall water treatment programme, including proper installation, maintenance and monitoring.

Key points to consider

- Have you assessed the risks and put suitable and sufficient controls in place?
- Do you have access to a competent person who can manage the risk from legionella?
- Do you ensure that the system remains clean, at the correct temperatures and there is no stagnation of water?
- Are the frequency of temperature checks and controls in line with HSE guidance? (See Table 2 above.)

Find out more

HSE's website on legionnaires' disease: www.hse.gov.uk/legionnaires

Legionnaires' disease: The control of legionella bacteria in water systems. Approved Code of Practice and guidance on regulations L8 (Fourth edition) HSE Books 2013 ISBN 978 0 7176 6615 7 www.hse.gov.uk/pubns/books/l8.htm

Legionnaires' disease: Control of legionella HSG274 HSE Books 2014 ISBN 978 0 7176 6635 5 www.hse.gov.uk/pubns/books/hsg274.htm

BS 7592:2008 *Sampling for legionella bacteria in water systems. Code of practice* British Standards Institution

Health Technical Memorandum 04-01 *The control of Legionella, hygiene, 'safe' hot water, cold water and drinking water systems:*
www.gov.uk/government/publications

Scottish Health Technical Memorandum 04-01 *The control of legionella, hygiene, 'safe' hot water, cold water and drinking water systems*
www.hfs.scot.nhs.uk/publications-1/engineering/shtm-04-01

Public Health England (PHE) Legionnaires' disease website (www.gov.uk/government/organisations/public-health-england) Provides information on legionnaires' disease and the requirement to report cases in England and Wales to PHE

HPS Scotland (www.hps.scot.nhs.uk) Provides information on legionnaires' disease and the requirement to report cases in Scotland to HPS

Chapter 10 Hot water and surfaces

10.1 Care homes often provide care for residents who may be vulnerable to risks from hot water or hot surfaces. Those at risk include people with reduced mental capacity or temperature sensitivity, and people who cannot react appropriately, or quickly enough, to prevent injury.

10.2 If hot water used for showering or bathing is above 44 °C, there is increased risk of serious injury or fatality. Where large areas of the body are exposed to high temperatures, scalds can be very serious and have led to fatalities.

10.3 Contact with surfaces above 43 °C can also lead to serious injury. This often occurs when residents fall and cannot move due to their condition or mobility, or are trapped by furniture. Incidents often occur in areas where there are low levels of supervision, eg in bedrooms, bathrooms and some communal areas.

10.4 When managing water temperatures to reduce the risk of scalding, you need to ensure that this does not compromise legionella control – see Chapter 9.

Key legislation

- Management of Health and Safety at Work Regulations 1999
- Provision and Use of Work Equipment Regulations 1998 (PUWER)

What you need to do

10.5 You should assess potential scalding and burning risks in the context of the vulnerability of those receiving care. A general assessment of the premises should identify what controls are necessary overall, and how the systems should be managed and maintained. This should then be supplemented by the inclusion of hot water and hot surface considerations in individuals' care assessments.

10.6 An individual's assessment needs to consider whether:

- the person's mental state means they cannot recognise or react to water or a surface that is too hot;
- the person is likely to try and run a bath or shower or add water when unattended;
- the person's lack of mobility means they are unable to respond safely to hot water or surfaces (eg safely getting in or out of the bath or shower, or moving away from a radiator);
- the person's sensitivity to temperature is impaired;
- the person can summon assistance;
- any lifting or other aids limit mobility in the bath or elsewhere;
- any furniture, fixtures and fittings restrict movement away from the source of heat.

10.7 The individual's assessment should detail any specific controls that are necessary to protect them.

Hot water

10.8 Where vulnerable residents are subject to whole-body immersion, widely recognised professional bathing practice involves testing water temperatures using a suitable thermometer to provide additional reassurance.

Controls

10.9 Suitable controls may include engineering controls to ensure that water is prevented from being discharged at greater than 44 °C from accessible outlets where there is potential for whole-body immersion.

10.10 Domestic electric showers are likely to have temperature regulation features but water temperatures above 44 °C may still occur if there are fluctuations in flow or pressure. If this is the case, and vulnerable people are at risk, additional measures will be required. Healthcare standard controls (eg thermostatic mixer valve (TMV) Type 3 or healthcare standard electric showers) and regular safety testing should ensure that the equipment remains safe at all times. TMVs should be located as close as possible to the outlet, where they are necessary, to help reduce the risk from legionella – see Chapter 9.

Hot surfaces

10.11 Most radiators, associated pipework and radiant electric heaters operate at temperatures that present a burn risk. Where vulnerable residents may come into prolonged contact with such equipment, it should be designed or covered so that the maximum accessible surface temperature does not exceed 43 °C.

Controls
10.12 The risk of burns from hot surfaces may be reduced by:

- providing heat emitters with low surface temperatures;
- locating sources of heat out of reach;
- guarding the heated areas (eg providing radiator covers or covering exposed pipework).

10.13 Where alterations are necessary, priority should be given to those surfaces where residents are most likely to sustain an injury, eg in bedrooms and bathrooms, or where residents may have difficulty moving away from the heat source.

Maintenance and monitoring
10.14 Controls should be adequately maintained to ensure they remain effective. Maintenance schedules should take into account local conditions (eg hard water or limescale), manufacturers' instructions and the risk of valve failure. Employees should be instructed to report any obvious defects immediately, and to take the facility out of use if necessary.

Key points to consider

- Have water temperatures, hot surfaces and the vulnerability of individuals been adequately assessed?
- Are suitable engineering controls provided, and are they effective?
- Are controls adequately maintained?

Find out more

Managing the risk from hot water and surfaces in health and social care
Health Services Information Sheet HSIS6 HSE 2012
www.hse.gov.uk/pubns/hsis6.htm

Controlling scalding risks from bathing and showering UK Homecare Association (UKHCA) Although this deals with caring for people in their own home, it provides good guidance on safe bathing procedures:
www.ukhca.co.uk/pdfs/bathingshowering.pdf

Chapter 11 Work-related violence and aggression

11.1 Both staff and residents have a right to expect a safe and secure environment. Incidents involving violence and aggression are one of the biggest causes of injuries reported under RIDDOR from the social care sector. These incidents don't always involve injury and the definition adopted for this publication is 'any incident in which a member of staff is verbally abused, threatened or assaulted by a resident or member of the public during the course of their work'.

Key legislation

- Management of Health and Safety at Work Regulations 1999

What you need to do

11.2 You should not expect your staff to accept incidents of violent or aggressive behaviour as a normal part of the job and you should work with them and residents to manage the risks.

11.3 The following are examples of aggression from challenging behaviour:

- a carer being bitten by a resident in the course of the normal care of that person;
- an angry visitor, who considers that their relative is not being properly treated, verbally abusing a manager;
- a carer being verbally abused and threatened by a resident who is unwilling to take prescribed medication;
- a confused resident striking out at a contractor repairing an item of equipment.

11.4 Residents may not deliberately set out to behave in a challenging way, and there may be an explanation. Staff who understand the reasons for such behaviour can usually work with the resident to manage it effectively for the benefit of all concerned. Some of the potential reasons for this behaviour can include:

- medication;
- frustration (due to problems communicating, or boredom);
- impatience (due to prolonged waiting, boredom or lack of information);
- anxiety (lack of choice or lack of space);
- resentment (lack of rights);
- medical condition and inherent aggression or mental instability.

11.5 If there is a risk from challenging behaviour in your care home, you need to manage it. The process for managing these risks may need to include general risks and risks from individuals.

The general risks

11.6 This should assess the overall level of risk, including:

- general risks to staff and other residents from residents, their relatives and visitors;
- the risks associated with the design of the work environment (eg blind spots, queuing points);
- the risks where homes provide different levels of care in different areas/units;
- the risks associated with lone working in the home or out on visits (see 'Find out more' at the end of the chapter for details of further advice on lone working).

The risks from individuals

11.7 Where individual residents pose a risk of aggression, an individual assessment should be completed and regularly reviewed as part of the care planning process. It should consider:

- the mental, emotional and physical condition of the resident;
- the effect of medical conditions and taking drugs, alcohol or medicines;
- their stress levels;
- whether they have a history of challenging, violent or aggressive behaviour and potential triggers for such behaviour;
- whether they consider others a threat.

11.8 There are a number of precautions that can help prevent and control challenging behaviour towards staff or others. Some examples are provided in the following paragraphs.

Work activities and communication

11.9 Consider the jobs people do and how they are done. For example, can you prevent cleaners and caterers coming into contact with residents that present challenging behaviour? You should:

- provide clear instructions;
- train staff to work safely with potentially aggressive or violent residents so they can, for example, recognise 'triggers';
- ensure suitable systems are in place for recording and exchanging information about residents and, where appropriate, their relatives (individual risk assessments, hand-over briefings, indicators on care plans, prompts in bedrooms);
- provide suitable staffing levels based on risk – certain times of the day may present a higher risk of challenging behaviour, eg bathing or meal times;
- have appropriate arrangements in place to respond to incidents and record them;
- manage new residents – check you have the right information at referral regarding violent behaviour and share it early with staff.

Work environment

11.10 Ensure the work environment is as safe and secure as possible to reduce the risk of aggression. The risks will vary depending on the services you provide, but you should consider:

- good visibility – open spaces and reduced trapping points;
- diffused and glare-free lighting;
- access to car parks and isolated areas;
- security systems such as fixed alarms or personal alarms.

11.11 It is difficult to manage the working environment when staff are expected to work away from the home, for example on day visits or trips. So it is especially important to assess the potential risks from challenging behaviour before any visit and consider working arrangements carefully.

Information and training

11.12 All staff likely to be exposed to potentially aggressive individuals should know and understand the preventive measures identified in their care plans. Pay particular attention when:

- new employees or agency workers are involved;
- new residents are admitted (especially those with a history of challenging behaviour);
- there has been a change in a person's mental or physical state, medication, behaviour, mood etc.

11.13 Training in preventing and managing violence and aggression can provide staff with appropriate skills to reduce or diffuse potential incidents. Such training should be available to all staff who come into contact with residents, including temporary or agency staff.

11.14 The right level of training should be identified through your risk assessment process. Basic training in the principles of managing challenging behaviour should include:

- causes of violence;
- recognition of warning signs;
- relevant interpersonal skills, ie verbal and non-verbal communication skills;
- de-escalation techniques;
- details of local working practices and control measures;
- incident reporting procedures.

11.15 All staff who may be exposed to challenging behaviour should receive the basic level of training. However, it is important to tailor the level and type of training provided to reflect the specific risks of the work activities, for example:

- staff caring for residents who present a low risk of aggressive behaviour may only require basic training;
- staff caring for residents with dementia may also need specific dementia awareness training, as well as basic training;
- staff caring for residents who present a serious risk of physical aggression may also need training in physical intervention techniques, as well as basic training.

11.16 Confidence and capability are important when dealing with an incident that involves potential aggression or violence; from time to time staff will need refresher training to update their skills. Training should be documented.

Helping staff after an incident

11.17 It can be useful to bring staff together after an incident to discuss what happened. This has two potential functions – to establish details of the event and to provide emotional help and support. It is sometimes appropriate to supplement debriefing with confidential counselling.

Key points to consider

- Has the risk of violence and aggression towards employees, or between residents, been assessed?
- Where necessary, are individual risk assessments completed and regularly reviewed as part of the care planning process?
- Do staff understand how different conditions, such as dementia, can present as challenging behaviour?
- Where appropriate, do staff receive training in recognising, tackling or avoiding violence and/or aggression?
- Are incidents of violence reported and followed up, and not just accepted as being 'part of the job'?
- Do you have a support process in place for those who suffer incidents of violence and aggression, eg counselling?

Find out more

HSE's webpage on violence and aggression in health and social care: www.hse.gov.uk/healthservices/violence

HSE's work-related violence website: www.hse.gov.uk/violence

Working alone: Health and safety guidance on the risks of lone working Leaflet INDG73(rev3) HSE Books 2013 www.hse.gov.uk/pubns/indg73.htm

Chapter 12 Work-related stress

12.1 Stress is 'the adverse reaction people have to excessive pressures or other types of demand placed on them at work'.

12.2 Pressure is part of work and keeps us motivated and productive. But too much pressure, or pressure that lasts for a long time, can lead to stress, which undermines performance, is costly to employers, and can damage both physical and mental health.

12.3 As an employer it is your duty to ensure, so far as is reasonably practicable, that your employees are not made ill by their work. Work-related stress can result in high staff turnover, an increase in sickness absence, reduced work performance, poor timekeeping and complaints.

Key legislation

- Management of Health and Safety at Work Regulations 1999

What you need to do

12.4 You should assess the risk by looking at available information, such as:

- feedback from staff and residents;
- sickness absence reports and fit notes;
- exit interviews from staff who are leaving;
- your own observations of how your staff are performing their jobs;
- asking them directly.

12.5 If you do not identify any issues with work-related stress at this stage, you may not need to do anything further apart from review as appropriate.

12.6 If you need to assess the risk further, the HSE Management Standards have been developed to help you deal with work-related stress. Small organisations may find it easier to simply use the principles of the Management Standards – discussing issues with employees and developing solutions – rather than using the indicator tool questionnaire.

12.7 Key to the Management Standards approach is working in partnership. Employers, employees and their representatives should work together to address potential sources of work-related stress throughout the organisation, and together develop sensible and cost-effective measures to tackle them. The Management Standards look at six principal areas:

- demands;
- control;
- support;
- relationships;
- role;
- change.

12.8 If you use a different approach to that set out in the Management Standards you can check your assessment is suitable and sufficient by using the HSE equivalence checklist (www.hse.gov.uk/stress/furtheradvice/equivalence.htm).

12.9 There is no single method for handling work-related stress. What you might need to do will depend on your working practices and the potential causes of the problem. However, only providing training, or help for sufferers, is unlikely to be effective as you will not actually tackle the source of the problem.

Table 3 Examples of how you might tackle stress at work

Problems that can lead to stress	What management can do
Doing the job	
The kind of support needed for particular residents	Change the way the jobs are done and move people between tasks
Lack of information on residents	Give staff as much information as possible
Working alone	Give warning of urgent or important jobs, prioritise tasks, stop unnecessary work
Inadequate resources and equipment	Provide relevant training
Responsibilities	
Poor management	Ensure everyone has clearly defined objectives and responsibilities
Confusion about roles	Provide training and support for those with responsibility for others
Having responsibility for looking after others	Monitor what's happening and provide positive and constructive feedback
Balancing work and home	
Irregular patterns of workdays	See if there is scope for flexible work schedules (eg flexible working hours)
Short notification of workdays	Plan work rotas well in advance
Relationships	
Poor relationship with others	Provide training in interpersonal skills
Bullying, racial or sexual harassment	Set up effective systems to prevent bullying and harassment (ensure there is a grievance procedure and investigation of complaints)
Working conditions	
Physical danger (eg hazardous chemicals, risk of violence) and poor general physical working conditions	Provide adequate control measures
	Ensure that working conditions and systems of work meet appropriate standards
Management behaviours	
Lack of control over work activities	Provide opportunities for staff to contribute ideas, especially in planning and organising their own jobs
Lack of communication and consultation	Introduce good communication, clear objectives, and close employee involvement, particularly during periods of change
Negative culture, eg a culture of blame when things go wrong, denial of potential problems	Be honest with yourself, set a good example, respect others and listen to them
Inability to discuss problems because of fear of criticism/reprisals	
Lack of support for individuals to develop their skills	Provide as much support as possible (eg leave, financial help) for staff to develop their skills. The Line Management Competency Tool can help with this: www.hse.gov.uk/stress/mcit.htm

12.10 You do not have to tackle stress caused by factors outside work, eg financial or domestic. However, these can make life difficult for people and their performance might suffer. Helping such employees may be in your interests.

12.11 Despite there being good arrangements in place to manage the risk, some individuals may still suffer from stress. Managers and colleagues are best placed to see many of the outward signs of stress in individuals. Look, in particular, for changes in the person's behaviour, such as deteriorating relationships with colleagues, irritability, indecisiveness, absenteeism or reduced performance. Those suffering from stress may smoke or drink alcohol more than usual. They might also complain about their health.

Key points to consider

- Have you assessed and managed potential causes of work-related stress, eg by using the Management Standards?
- Have you worked with your employees and their representatives to tackle the issues?
- Do you take action if employees are showing signs of work-related stress?

Find out more

HSE's work-related stress website: www.hse.gov.uk/stress

How to tackle work-related stress: A guide for employers on making the Management Standards work Leaflet INDG430 HSE Books 2009 www.hse.gov.uk/pubns/indg430.pdf

Working together to reduce stress at work: A guide for employees Leaflet INDG424 HSE Books 2008 www.hse.gov.uk/pubns/indg424.pdf

The nature, causes and consequences of harm in emotionally-demanding occupations Prepared by Birbeck College, University of London, for HSE 2008 www.hse.gov.uk/research/rrpdf/rr610.pdf

Chapter 13 General working environment

13.1 Care homes aim to provide a homely and welcoming environment for their residents. However, they are also workplaces and, while making the care home environment comfortable for residents, providers must also comply with workplace law.

Key legislation

- Workplace (Health, Safety and Welfare) Regulations 1992
- Control of Asbestos Regulations 2012
- Control of Substances Hazardous to Health Regulations 2002
- Personal Protective Equipment at Work Regulations 1992
- Gas Safety (Installation and Use) Regulations 1998
- Health and Safety (Display Screen Equipment) Regulations 1992

13.2 Some of these specific regulations only apply to employees. However, you as an employer have a general duty to ensure that the premises are safe for everyone who uses them, so far as reasonably practicable.

What you need to do

Asbestos

13.3 If you own, manage or have responsibilities for a care home or an associated building that may contain asbestos, you need to think about the risks of asbestos exposure to employees and others who may use the building.

13.4 It is your job to manage that risk, and provide information on where any asbestos is and what condition it is in. If you have no or limited information on the building, an asbestos survey is a good way of identifying its location and condition. Alternatively, if you need to disturb the material, you can just assume it does contain asbestos and take the appropriate precautions for the highest-risk situation.

13.5 Asbestos is likely to be present if the building was constructed or refurbished between 1950 and 2000, particularly if it also has a steel frame and/or boilers with thermal insulation. Owners, managers and maintenance staff need the following information about asbestos, which should be recorded and easily accessible:

- its location;
- the type of material (lagging, ceiling tiles, partition board etc);
- its condition;
- the type of asbestos (blue, brown or white).

13.6 If asbestos is in poor condition or it is likely to be damaged or disturbed, it should be repaired, sealed, enclosed or removed. You will need to seek specialist advice from a contractor licensed by HSE on the appropriate action to take.

13.7 If the asbestos is in good condition, not likely to be damaged and not likely to be worked on, it is safe to leave in place, then a management system will need to be introduced The management system should periodically check that the asbestos is correctly labelled, remains in good condition and has not been damaged.

13.8 People working in and around asbestos are often inadvertently exposed (electricians, plumbers, maintenance staff etc). They must be informed of the presence of asbestos before being allowed to start work. If a contractor is being used, you need to understand their proposed safe system of work so that you can be confident that their precautions will adequately protect employees and residents from exposure.

Find out more
HSE's asbestos website: www.hse.gov.uk/asbestos

Managing and working with asbestos: Control of Asbestos Regulations 2012. Approved Code of Practice and guidance L143 (Second edition) HSE Books 2013 ISBN 978 0 7176 6618 8 www.hse.gov.uk/pubns/books/l143.htm

Managing asbestos in buildings: A brief guide Leaflet INDG223(rev5) HSE Books 2012 www.hse.gov.uk/pubns/indg223.htm

Radon

13.9 Radon is a naturally occurring radioactive gas that can seep out of the ground and build up in houses and indoor workplaces located in a 'radon-affected area'. Information on whether your care home is located in a radon affected area, and the degree of likely risk, can be found on the UK radon website (www.ukradon.org).

13.10 The highest levels are usually found in underground spaces such as basements. High concentrations can also be found in groundfloor buildings because they are usually at slightly lower pressure than the surrounding atmosphere, allowing radon from the sub-soil to enter through cracks and gaps in the floor, if appropriate precautions are not taken.

13.11 Radon assessments should be carried out in any building or basement where its location and characteristics suggest that elevated levels may be found and significant exposures to employees and/or other people are possible. This could apply to care homes, as they are occupied by employees and residents for long periods. Assessment is needed for all workplaces below ground and all workplaces in radon-affected areas. Inexpensive surveys can be carried out by leaving small, plastic, passive detectors in appropriate locations.

Find out more
HSE webpage on radon in the workplace:
www.hse.gov.uk/radiation/ionising/radon.htm

UK Radon website (the UK reference site on radon from Public Health England): www.ukradon.org

Gas safety

13.12 Gas appliances, and associated pipework, flues and ventilation, should be checked for safety at least once a year by Gas Safe registered engineers. Servicing at the same time is advisable, to ensure they are maintained in a safe condition. Registered engineers must carry out any work on gas appliances and pipework. Liquefied petroleum gas (LPG) installations and service pipework should also be inspected and maintained to ensure that thay are in a safe condition.

Find out more
HSE webpage on gas safety: www.hse.gov.uk/toolbox/gas.htm

Safety in the installation and use of gas systems and appliances: Gas Safety (Installation and Use) Regulations 1998. Approved Code of Practice and guidance L56 (Fourth edition) HSE Books 2013 ISBN 978 0 7176 6617 1 www.hse.gov.uk/pubns/books/l56.htm

Gas appliances: Get them checked – Keep them safe Leaflet INDG238(rev3) HSE Books 2009 www.hse.gov.uk/pubns/indg238.pdf

Fire safety

13.13 General fire precautions, eg ensuring adequate means of escape from a building, are enforced by individual Fire and Rescue Services in England, Wales and Scotland. HSE deals with process fire risk, eg using flammable liquids and LPG or electrical faults, which can cause fires.

13.14 Although serious fires in care homes are fairly rare, when they do occur they can be catastrophic. Therefore, those responsible for the premises (eg employers and/or building owners or occupiers) must take precautions to prevent fire.

13.15 Those responsible for the premises must carry out a fire safety risk assessment, keep it up to date, and use it to ensure that necessary fire safety measures are in place. It should identify what could cause a fire to start, including:

- sources of ignition (eg heat or sparks);
- materials that burn;
- people who may be at risk.

13.16 Simple control measures include:

- keeping sources of ignition and flammable substances apart;
- ensuring good housekeeping (eg avoid build-up of rubbish);
- considering how to detect fires and how to warn people quickly if they start – special arrangements may be required where residents have mobility issues;
- having the correct fire-fighting equipment, ensuring these are correctly maintained;
- keeping fire exits and escape routes clearly marked and unobstructed;
- ensuring your workers receive appropriate training.

Find out more
HSE webpage on fire safety: www.hse.gov.uk/toolbox/fire.htm

National government websites:
www.communities.gov.uk/firesafety
www.wales.gov.uk/topics/housingandcommunity/safety/fire
www.scotland.gov.uk/topics/justice/policies/police-fire-rescue

Contractors

13.17 Contractors can include window cleaners, gardeners and contract cleaners. Both you and the contractor have responsibility for health and safety and it is important to take the right precautions to reduce the risks to your employees, the contractor's employees and others in the care home.

13.18 When selecting suitable contractors you should consider the following points:

- Can the contractor do this job safely?
- Have you and the contractor assessed the risks of the work, shared this with each other and agreed how to manage these risks?
- Have you informed your employees about what to expect, and what they may need to do?
- Have you arrangements in hand for supervision and coordination during the work?

Find out more
HSE web page on contractors: www.hse.gov.uk/toolbox/workers/contractors.htm

Using contractors: A brief guide Leaflet INDG368(rev1) HSE Books 2012 www.hse.gov.uk/pubns/indg368.htm

Outside areas and vehicle movements

13.19 It may be necessary to establish whether garden and outdoor areas, such as ponds, steps/paths, greenhouses, swimming pools or balconies, can pose a significant risk to vulnerable residents and visitors. You should consider ways of managing the risks to vunerable people so they can still enjoy the outdoor environment and their participation in activities is not unduly restricted.

13.20 The movement of vehicles around your care home can be a risk to residents, visitors and employees. When assessing the risks you should consider three key areas:

- *Are the outside areas safe?* Have you assessed the safety of vehicle routes and speeds, parking, lighting, location and unloading of deliveries, visibility and signage, driving surfaces and segregating people and vehicles?
- *Is the vehicle safe?* If you have work vehicles, eg for transporting residents, are they safe for their intended use?
- *Are people safe?* Do visitors and contractors follow the arrangements you have in place, and are employees safe to transport residents?

Find out more
HSE's workplace transport web page: www.hse.gov.uk/toolbox/transport.htm

Workplace transport safety: An employers' guide HSG136 (Second edition) HSE Books 2005 ISBN 978 0 7176 6154 1 www.hse.gov.uk/pubns/books/hsg136.htm

Workplace transport safety: A brief guide Leaflet INDG199(rev2) HSE Books 2013 www.hse.gov.uk/pubns/indg199.htm

Doors and gates

13.21 Doors and gates in areas of the building where residents have access should be designed so they can be opened easily and should not be fitted with strong self-closers. In some instances, where it does not cause an obstruction, it might be beneficial to re-hang some doors to open outwards, eg in toilets and bathrooms, as this improves access for emergencies and for moving and handling. Consider how staff can gain emergency access to areas where they may need to assist a lone resident, eg toilets and bathrooms. Locks that can be overridden by staff in the event of emergencies may be appropriate for such areas.

13.22 The security of doors and gates should be considered where your assessment identifies that specific residents leaving the premises will present a significant risk to their safety. In some instances it may be appropriate to consider devices that alert staff of their location and whether they are at risk of harm.

13.23 As with all issues around the design of a building, your assessment should consider the types of doors and closers required for fire protection, and the advice of a fire safety officer may be required.

Find out more
Workplace health, safety and welfare. Workplace (Health, Safety and Welfare) Regulations 1992. Approved Code of Practice and guidance L24 (Second edition) HSE Books 2013 ISBN 978 0 7176 6583 9 www.hse.gov.uk/pubns/books/l24.htm

Workplace health, safety and welfare: A short guide for managers Leaflet INDG244(rev2) HSE Books 2007 www.hse.gov.uk/pubns/indg244.htm

Ventilation and heating

13.24 Workplaces need to be adequately ventilated with fresh, clean air. However, you should provide an environment that is comfortable and suitable for their residents as well as staff. Windows or other openings may provide sufficient ventilation, but the risks of residents falling must also be considered, as explained in Chapter 7.

13.25 Where fumes or hot equipment may be present, such as in the laundry or kitchen, more fresh air is likely to be needed to remove fumes and control humidity and temperature. Where necessary, additional ventilation systems should be provided and regularly maintained.

Find out more
HSE's web page on ventilation: www.hse.gov.uk/toolbox/harmful/ventilation.htm

Display screen equipment (DSE)

13.26 The main risks that may arise in work with DSE are musculoskeletal disorders such as back pain or upper limb disorders (sometimes known as repetitive strain injury or RSI), visual fatigue, and mental stress.

13.27 You should assess workstations that are regularly used, and assess and reduce risks. Look at the workstation (including equipment, furniture, and the work environment), the range of work being done, any special needs of individual staff and, where risks are identified, take steps to reduce them.

Find out more
HSE's display screen equipment (DSE) webpages: www.hse.gov.uk/msd/dse

Working with display screen equipment (DSE): A brief guide Leaflet INDG36(rev4) HSE Books 2013 www.hse.gov.uk/pubns/indg36.htm

Key points to consider

- Have you carried out an assessment of the premises, and do you regularly check they are in good repair?
- Do you know whether there are asbestos-containing materials in your premises and, if so, do you have a system for controlling the risks?
- Is your care home located in a radon-affected area? If so, then have you arranged for an assessment to be carried out?
- Are utilities, such as gas, properly maintained?
- How do you check that any contractors you use are competent and do not put your staff and residents at risk?
- Have you assessed the risks from outside areas and the risks of vehicles moving around the premises?
- Have DSE workstations been assessed and, where risks have been identified, have actions been taken to reduce them?

Chapter 14 General welfare

14.1 This chapter covers the range of welfare requirements that apply to a care home. As mentioned in the previous chapter, the aim is to ensure that care homes can provide a homely environment while ensuring that the welfare of employees is safeguarded.

Key legislation

- Workplace (Health, Safety and Welfare) Regulations 1992
- Health and Safety (First-Aid) Regulations 1981
- Working Time (Amendment) Regulations 2009

14.2 While these generally only apply to the safety etc of employees, employers also have a general duty under other legislation to ensure that the premises are safe for everyone, so far as reasonably practicable.

What you need to do

Staff welfare facilities

14.3 You must ensure you provide suitable toilets, washing facilities, rest facilities and changing facilities for people at work.

14.4 Sufficient toilets and washing facilities should be provided for the maximum number of people likely to be at work at any one time (see Table 4 below). Toilets should be clean, well-lit, adequately ventilated and supplied with hot and cold water, soap and drying facilities. Provide means for disposing of sanitary dressings where women use toilets.

14.5 Men and women should have separate facilities unless the toilet is in a separate room for use by one person at a time, with a lockable door. Generally, employees should have separate toilet facilities to those provided for residents, but in small care homes this may not be practicable.

Table 4 Number of facilities needed per number of people at work

Number of people at work	Number of toilets	Number of wash basins
1–5	1	1
6–25	2	2
26–50	3	3

14.6 Changing areas and facilities for storing clothing should be provided if employees need to change into work clothing on the premises, eg if kitchen or nursing staff are required to change into uniforms for hygiene and infection control reasons.

14.7 Rest facilities with seating should be provided for employees to take breaks. They should have access to a facility to obtain drinking water, and prepare a hot drink. Where meals are eaten at work there should be a place for employees to eat with clean surfaces on which food can be placed. For those working during out of hours or in locations where hot food cannot be obtained, there should be facilities for storing and heating their own food.

Find out more
Workplace health, safety and welfare. Workplace (Health, Safety and Welfare) Regulations 1992. Approved Code of Practice and guidance L24 (Second edition) HSE Books 2013 ISBN 978 0 7176 6583 9 www.hse.gov.uk/pubns/books/l24.htm

Workplace health, safety and welfare: A short guide for managers Leaflet INDG244(rev2) HSE Books 2007 www.hse.gov.uk/pubns/indg244.htm

HSE webpage on providing the right workplace facilities: www.hse.gov.uk/simple-health-safety/workplace.htm

Smoking

14.8 Care homes are allowed to have designated rooms that are only used for residents' smoking, but there is no legal obligation for them to offer such designated smoking rooms if they do not wish to do so. You therefore need to properly consult with staff and residents to establish an overall policy on smoking.

14.9 If designated rooms are provided, this will mean that non-smokers could be in close contact with residents who smoke, so you must reduce employees' and non-smokers' risk from second-hand smoke to as low a level as reasonably practicable. Ways you can achieve this include:

- taking residents' smoking practices and history into account when allocating bedrooms;
- banning smoking in all common areas such as corridors, lifts and dining rooms;
- designating separate smoking and non-smoking common rooms;
- improving ventilation/extraction systems so that smoke is effectively removed from the designated smoking areas of the care home.

14.10 Cleaning and other access to rooms where smoking is allowed will be difficult to manage, and this is an issue where staff consultation is essential.

14.11 Local authorities are responsible for enforcing smokefree legislation. Responsibility for enforcing fire safety legislation, including judgements about its application, is a matter for the fire authorities. If you have queries regarding fire safety you can contact your local fire safety officer.

Find out more
HSE advice on smoking at work: www.hse.gov.uk/contact/faqs/smoking.htm

Working time

14.12 Although the Working Time Regulations do not come under the HSWA, it may be helpful for employers to be aware of the duties so we have included them here for information. The basic rights and protections that the Working Time Regulations provide for workers are:

- a limit of an average of 48 hours a week which a worker can be required to work (though workers can choose to work more if they want to);
- for night workers, an average of 8 hours work in each 24-hour period (calculated over the appropriate reference period);

- the right for night workers to receive free health assessments;
- the right to 11 hours consecutive rest a day;
- the right to a day off each week;
- the right to a rest break if the working day is longer than six hours;
- the right to four weeks' paid leave per year.

14.13 A worker is someone who has a contract of employment, or someone who is paid a regular salary or wage and works for an organisation, business or individual. Workers can agree to work longer than the 48-hour limit. An agreement must be in writing and signed by the worker. This is generally referred to as an opt-out. It can be for a specified period or an indefinite period. You as an employer cannot force a worker to sign an opt-out. Workers cannot be dismissed or subjected to detriment for refusing to sign an opt-out.

Young workers

14.14 Young workers have special rights under the Working Time Regulations. The rights of young workers (those over the minimum school leaving age but under 18) and those under the minimum school age on approved work experience schemes differ in the following ways:

- a limit of eight hours working time a day and 40 hours a week (unless there are special circumstances);
- not to work either between 10 pm and 6 am or between 11 pm and 7 am (except in certain circumstances);
- 12 hours' rest between each working day;
- two days' weekly rest and a 30-minute in-work rest break when working longer than four and a half hours.

Night workers

14.15 To be sure workers are fit for night work, you must offer a free health assessment to anyone who is about to start working nights and to all night workers on a regular basis, as appropriate. A night worker cannot opt-out of the average of 8 hours in a 24-hour period, although there are exceptions in healthcare where there is a need for continuity of service. Where a night worker's work involves special hazards or heavy physical or mental strain, there is an absolute limit of 8 hours on their working time each 24-hour period – this is not an average.

14.16 HSE and local authorities are responsible for the enforcement of the maximum weekly working time limit, night work limits and health assessments for night work. Rest and leave entitlements are enforced through employment tribunals.

Find out more
HSE webpages on the Working Time Regulations:
www.hse.gov.uk/contact/faqs/workingtimedirective.htm

Advice from gov.uk: www.gov.uk/maximum-weekly-working-hours

Department of Business, Innovation and Skills: www.bis.gov.uk

New and expectant mothers

14.17 You should assess risks to all employees, taking into account any specific risks to females of childbearing age who could become pregnant, and control these risks so far as reasonably practicable.

14.18 If an employee notifies you in writing that she is pregnant, has given birth in the previous six months or is breastfeeding, you must consider any further risks to that employee, in addition to those identified in the initial risk assessment. You have a duty to regularly monitor and review any assessment made to take into account possible risks that may occur at different stages of the pregnancy.

14.19 You have the right to request a certificate from your employee's GP or midwife to prove that she is pregnant. If an employee fails to produce a certificate within a reasonable amount of time, then you are under no obligation to implement special control measures.

14.20 If any risks are identified which go beyond the level of risk found outside the workplace, then you must take the following actions to remove the pregnant employee from those risks:

- **Action 1:** temporarily adjust her working conditions and/or hours of work, unless it is not reasonable to do so, or would not avoid the risk;
- **Action 2:** offer her suitable alternative work (at the same rate of pay) if available, or if that is not feasible;
- **Action 3:** suspend her from work on paid leave for as long as necessary to protect her health and safety, and that of her child.

14.21 Where a new or expectant mother works nights and provides a medical certificate from her GP or midwife which says that working night shifts will affect her health, then you must suspend her from that work, on full pay, for as long as necessary. However, the Employment Rights Act 1996 provide that, where appropriate, employers should offer suitable alternative work, on the same terms and conditions, before any suspension from work is considered.

Find out more
HSE webpages on new and expectant mothers: www.hse.gov.uk/mothers

New and expectant mothers who work: A brief guide to your health and safety Leaflet INDG373(rev2) HSE Books 2013 www.hse.gov.uk/pubns/indg373.htm

First aid

14.22 You are required to provide adequate and appropriate equipment, facilities and personnel to ensure that employees receive immediate attention if they are injured or taken ill at work. This applies to all workplaces including those with fewer than five employees. There is no legal obligation for care homes to make first-aid provision for non-employees, such as those residents and visitors, but it clearly makes sense to include residents and others when thinking about the overall level of first-aid provision needed.

14.23 However, if training in emergency techniques would be appropriate to control or mitigate risk, for example if residents are known to be at serious risk of choking, then such training may be required under the HSWA.

14.24 The following table, based on HSE guidance on first-aid provision for employees, indicates the kind of ratios that might be appropriate in medium-risk premises such as a care home. This can be used directly as a guide for statutory first-aid provision for employees, or more widely when considering the overall level of first-aid provision that the care home may choose to provide.

Table 5 Ratios of first-aid personnel to employees

From your risk assessment, what degree of hazard is associated with your work activities?	How many employees do you have?	What first-aid personnel do you need?
Medium-risk (eg most care homes)	Fewer than 5	At least one appointed person
	5–50	At least one first-aider trained in EFAW or FAW depending on the type of injuries that might occur
	More than 50	At least one first-aider trained in FAW for every 50 employed (or part thereof)

14.25 First-aiders are those who have undertaken training appropriate to the circumstances. They must hold a valid certificate of competence in either:

- first aid at work (FAW);
- emergency first aid at work (EFAW);
- any other level of training or qualification that is appropriate to the circumstances.

14.26 If you decide a first-aider is not required in the care home, a person should be appointed to take charge of the first-aid arrangements. The role of this appointed person includes looking after the first-aid equipment and facilities and calling the emergency services when required. To fulfil their role, the appointed person does not need first-aid training, though emergency first-aid training may be beneficial.

Find out more
HSE's first aid site: www.hse.gov.uk/firstaid

First aid at work: The Health and Safety (First-Aid) Regulations 1981. Guidance on Regulations L74 (Third edition) HSE Books 2013 ISBN 978 0 7176 6560 0 www.hse.gov.uk/pubns/books/l74.htm

First aid at work: Your questions answered Leaflet INDG214(rev2) HSE Books 2014 www.hse.gov.uk/pubns/indg214.htm

Key points to consider

- Do you provide adequate welfare facilities for your staff?
- Do you have a policy on smoking, and do you effectively reduce second-hand smoke exposure if smoking is allowed?
- Do you have records showing compliance with working time limits?
- Do you have arrangements in place to consider the risks to new and expectant mothers?
- Have you made adequate arrangements for first-aid provision?

Appendix 1 Legal framework

The Health and Safety at Work etc Act 1974 (HSWA)

A1 The HSWA is the primary legislation covering occupational health and safety in the United Kingdom. It sets out the general duties that employers have towards employees and members of the public, and employees have to themselves and to each other.

Duties of employers to employees

A2 Employers have a general duty under the HSWA to ensure the health, safety and welfare at work of all their employees. This duty is qualified in the Act by the principle of 'so far as reasonably practicable'. This means balancing the level of risk against the measures needed to control the real risk in terms of money, time or trouble. However, you do not need to take action if it would be grossly disproportionate to the level of risk (www.hse.gov.uk/risk/faq.htm).

Duties of employers to people who are not in their employment

A3 Employers and self-employed people have a general duty under the HSWA, so far as reasonably practicable, to protect the health, safety and welfare of people who might be affected by their business. These include residents in a care home, visitors, volunteers, and contractors' employees working on their premises. Examples of where people may be affected by the work activity are:

- safety risks to people using the service, eg scalding, falls from windows, bed-rail entrapment etc;
- users of the care service being injured during moving and handling;
- contractors and visitors being exposed to risks, eg from asbestos, because they have not being informed of safety-critical issues;
- injuries caused by vehicle movements on the premises.

Duties of employees

A4 Employees have a general duty under the HSWA to take reasonable care of their own health and safety and that of others who may be affected by what they do or fail to do, and to cooperate with their employer.

A5 In addition, they must not intentionally or recklessly interfere with or misuse anything required by the HSWA for the health, safety or welfare of themselves, residents or others.

A6 If you have staff whose first language is not English, you need to ensure that they understand health and safety procedures and the instructions and training they are being given. They must also be able to communicate any concerns they have.

Duties of directors and senior managers

A7 Where an offence is committed with the consent or connivance of a director, manager, secretary or other similar officer of a health or social care provider, or where it is committed due to their neglect, they are liable to prosecution. For example, if a director of a care provider allows a clearly unsafe practice, which is in breach of legislation, he or she may be guilty of an offence.

Find out more

Health and safety regulation: A short guide Leaflet HSC13(rev1) HSE Books 2003 www.hse.gov.uk/pubns/hsc13.htm

Health and safety made simple: The basics for your business Leaflet INDG449 HSE Books 2011 www.hse.gov.uk/pubns/indg449.htm
Microsite: www.hse.gov.uk/simple-health-safety

The health and safety toolbox: How to control risks at work HSG268 HSE Books 2013 ISBN 978 0 7176 6447 4 www.hse.gov.uk/pubns/books/hsg268.htm
Microsite: www.hse.gov.uk/toolbox

Further information

For information about health and safety, or to report inconsistencies or inaccuracies in this guidance, visit www.hse.gov.uk. You can view HSE guidance online and order priced publications from the website. HSE priced publications are also available from bookshops.

British Standards can be obtained in PDF or hard copy formats from BSI: http://shop.bsigroup.com or by contacting BSI Customer Services for hard copies only Tel: 0845 086 9001 email: cservices@bsigroup.com.

The Stationery Office publications are available from The Stationery Office, PO Box 29, Norwich NR3 1GN Tel: 0870 600 5522 Fax: 0870 600 5533 email: customer.services@tso.co.uk Website: www.tsoshop.co.uk. (They are also available from bookshops.) Statutory Instruments can be viewed free of charge at www.legislation.gov.uk where you can also search for changes to legislation.

This publication is available at www.hse.gov.uk/pubns/books/hsg220.htm.